A HISTORY OF THE FRENCH LANGUAGE

BY

URBAN T. HOLMES, JR.
UNIVERSITY OF NORTH CAROLINA

AND

ALEXANDER H. SCHUTZ
THE OHIO STATE UNIVERSITY

BIBLO and TANNEN
NEW YORK
1967

ORIGINALLY PUBLISHED 1938
REPRINTED 1967
BY
BIBLO and TANNEN BOOKSELLERS and PUBLISHERS, INC.
63 FOURTH AVENUE   NEW YORK, NEW YORK 10003

Library of Congress Catalog Card Number 67-19528

Printed in the United States of America

PREFACE

The best definition of Culture is to define it as an understanding of human experience. No man, if he lived to be a centenarian, could absorb from actual experience, or contact with life, the judgments and observations which should be commonplace to any one versed in the humanities and the sciences. We go to the university to grow old in wisdom before our years. Just as history and literature reflect the development of the peoples of the past ages so does an understanding of language. Language and its changes through the centuries are as faithful a record of human mentality as the modern phonograph record is of human sound. It is to suggest this new vista in the comprehension of the French people that this book has been written.

Although Plato and his predecessors in ancient Greece were interested in tracing the history of words, an interest which remained alive through succeeding centuries and even fascinated such a thinker as Dante, no formal progress in scientific linguistics was possible before the late eighteenth century. The first important scientific discovery which paved the way for linguistic study was a result of the conquest of India: it became evident that Sanskrit, the sacred language of India, and Latin and Greek were related. Thus Indo-European linguistics was born, and then was scientifically established by Franz Bopp (1791–1867). Bopp inspired the Grimm brothers to investigate the laws of Germanic linguistics; Jacob Grimm (1785–1863) and Wilhelm von Humboldt (1767–1836) inspired Friedrich Diez to lay the foundations for Romance Philology. We have just celebrated the one-hundredth anniversary of the publication of Diez's *Grammatik der romanischen Sprachen* (1836). It was Gaston Paris (1839–1903) and Paul Meyer (1840–1917) who introduced the scientific study of the Romance languages into France; and it was A. Marshall Elliott (1846–1910) who furthered the spread of this science in America.

Many masters have followed in the footsteps of the pioneers and it is our hope that the pages of the book which we present will condense some of their discoveries into a readable but accurate form. Our readers will necessarily be of two types: those who are

following an undergraduate course in this subject and those who
desire specialized knowledge. There are certain sections of our
book, such as sections (5), (10A), (16), and (17) which might be
omitted in undergraduate courses. Critics will understand that
throughout this manual the material has been condensed to suit the
needs of a semester course meeting three hours a week.

The authors should be pardoned if they occasionally speak of the
French language as though it were capable of existing and acquiring
influence by itself. A language, of course, exists only in books and
in the minds of its speakers. In the matter of linguistic change we
personally do not hold with the so-called *Junggrammatiker* of Leipzig
(1872 on) who believed that sound laws are natural laws. The
speakers of a given language, during the ancient world and the
Middle Ages, were grouped into a large number of small communities, each centering around its market town. All of the speakers
tended to modify their language according to a certain program or
"drift" inherent in the language and in their national outlook,
but these modifications were not constant in time or extent throughout the individual groups. More important communities tended to
influence adjacent smaller groups, and the speech of the king's
court, or of some great center, was apt to exercise a leveling process
over all the groups — the inevitable result of language change
under such circumstances as these can only be a multitude of dialects of the one dominant language. When we speak of the French
language today we mean the standard literary language which is a
polished form of the dialect which developed in and near Paris.
For a view of the other dialects which are still current over the
territory of France one has only to consult the ALF or *Atlas linguistique de la France* (Paris: Champion, 1902–1915) of Gilliéron
and Edmont. Many dialect dictionaries have been compiled for the
individual modern dialects. An excellent bibliography of these
dictionaries is von Wartburg's *Bibliographie des dictionnaires patois*
(Paris: Droz, 1934). To facilitate the use of this bibliography in
the United States G. C. S. Adams and C. M. Woodard have issued
a *Census of French and Provençal Dialect Dictionaries in American
Libraries* (Ling. Soc. of America, 1937).

At the end of each chapter we have suggested works of reference
that will furnish all the detailed bibliography required and which
can be used for outside reading. We warn the instructor of an
undergraduate class in this subject, however, that outside reading
should not be emphasized except for students of a special type.

Such a class for undergraduates is only an orientation course, and most of the literature on linguistic topics is highly technical. The authors have in preparation a source book which will provide illustrative material with ample notes.

Other manuals dealing with the history of the French language, from varying points of view, are: W. von Wartburg's *Evolution et structure de la langue française* (Paris: Droz, 1933, and Univ. of Chicago Press, 1937), Albert Dauzat's *Histoire de la langue française* (Paris: Payot, 1930), A. Loiseau's *Histoire de la langue française* (Paris: Boccard), and A. Ewert's *The French Language* (London: Faber & Faber, 1933). Students may be referred also to Chapter One of C. Nyrop's *Gramm. histor. langue frçse.* (Copenhagen, 1914), I, and to the monumental *Histoire de la langue française* of Ferdinand Brunot (1860–1938), *q. v. infra.*

The portion of this book devoted to the Introduction and to the French language before 1600 is largely the work of U. T. Holmes; the field from 1600 to the present day has been covered by A. H. Schutz. Each collaborator, however, is jointly responsible for the whole. This manual has been issued in three mimeographed editions since 1933, and has reached its present form after classroom use in three universities.

TABLE OF CONTENTS

A History of the French Language

I

INTRODUCTION

1. LANGUAGE

Many thinkers have reached the conclusion that language and reason in man are one and the same thing. That is, without language man's thoughts would be reduced to the simplest expression of emotion and desire by bodliy signs; he would be but little better than a dog or other higher animal. If this be true, in the study of language lies a key for the solution of evolution, psychology, and many other ologies about mankind which have beset the scientists for ages. The natural sciences — chemistry, physics, and biology — still contain many mysteries, but their devotees stand on far firmer ground than the philosopher, the psychologist, and the anthropologist. Man is still the great mystery, and it is not too vain to hope that some day language students may be able to offer a beginning to a solution of the mystery.[1]

Various theories have been offered to explain, not the efficient cause necessarily, but the first manifestations of human language. There is the so-called " bow-wow " theory, held by the ancient Epicurean philosophers, and by the modern Jean-Jacques Rousseau: that the first intelligible sounds were interjections and that these developed fixed associations from frequent repetition. There is the " ding-dong " theory, which was believed by the ancient Stoïcs and by the German poet and philosopher Herder: that first words were onomatopoetic, that they sought to imitate sounds heard. Far more understandable is the belief now commonly held: that the tongue and lip muscles being naturally mobile, primitive man soon found that air pressure, released through them under emotional stress, produced tones varying in quality. As a result the intoning of meaningless and even indistinct sounds became a habit with him

---

[1] Bloomfield in *Studies in Philology*, XXVII, 553 ff.

as his emotions rose and fell when he labored in the fields, hunted, or fought. Gradually the primitive individuals of a given social group began to narrow down the multiplicity of these emotional outpourings to combinations of some sixty sounds, and quickening intelligences associated certain combinations with certain tasks and certain conditions. As mentality continued to develop there was a drift towards short cuts, towards further simplification, and language has continued that drift through all its centuries of history till the present day. The history of a language appears to be a survey of how it has ironed out its complications, from that early dawn where expression was multiple in its vagueness till the time when logic and writing have made of it a subtle, precise, and powerful instrument.

Early language did not know what we call words — a splitting up of an utterance into single concept units — man's power of analysis had not yet gone that far. The first single concepts of which primitive men became conscious were larger groups or agglutinations which we should define as a predication closely bound up with its immediate modifiers; compare the modern Eskimo *takusariar-torumagaluranerpa* " do you think he really intends to bother with it ? " which is a concept reduced to its simplest form for an Eskimo. If this happened to be the last element in an address by an Eskimo and if he were asked to repeat the last word, he would repeat this whole combination. Primitive men of the present-day world are far from being similar to mankind in his cradle, but their languages often have not developed as far as those spoken for centuries by men of a more advanced civilization. We can cite such languages in our historical discussions, with reservations.

Language, which began as the involuntary emotional reactions of individuals, was soon socialized by daily intercourse among individuals of the same group and it accomplished its most practical result, intercommunication between individuals. Members of a given group now had a vehicle which allowed the expression of wants and needs to a neighbor, but best of all they had the means of communing within themselves — and this must have been the greatest and one of the longest steps of progress to be realized. The entity of the Person which, in plain language, means the ability to reflect — to go back over past experience, to exercise judgment — is the enigma which we want so much to solve and which we believe to be closely tied up with the process of self-communication and expression. Once this ability was realized, men of definite groups developed spiritually and mentally along definite lines, and this newly discovered mental development reflected itself in the language development. Language drift and mental outlook of a group are closely bound, each influencing the other: to understand either one of them some account must be taken of the other.

2. INDO-EUROPEAN

We still know very little about ethnic groups or racial stocks, but we do know that a large group of individuals speaking the same language, whom we conveniently call the Indo-Europeans, were resident in North Central Europe in 3000 B.C. (Many scholars refuse to accept Northern Europe as the early Indo-European habitat; southern European Russia suits them better.)[2] These people did not write and it is probable that their religion did not allow them to record their poetry and sacred lore, if we can judge from the later Celtic druids. The group doubtless grew to be considerable in numbers and we may suppose that its members began to spread a little apart quite early; this would bring about petty divergences of speech, or dialects, even in this early Indo-European. By 2000 B.C. or slightly earlier a contingent of these people began to migrate to more distant fields, passing the Hellespont and through Asia Minor; they finally settled in India and the Iranian plateau. Other tribes who show close relation to this first daring horde of migrators settled in the Caucasus and Asia, the Tokharians, the Armenians, and possibly the Hittites. Another group whom we have come to call the Achaean Greeks moved into Greece, followed by the Albanians, who did not enter the Greek peninsula. Most important for us is another large unit of the Indo-European peoples who apparently did not migrate for a considerable time and who formed a dialect unity among themselves: the Balto-Slavonic speakers, the Germanic, and the Italo-Celtic. If we can imagine them expanding away from the center, the following diagram should be of use.

Movement is indicated by the line; Stage II left the Balto-Slavonic peoples behind, Stage III left the Germanic and so forth,

[2] S. Feist in *Language*, VIII, 245 ff.

until finally the Osco-Umbrians and the Latins, together (IV), entered the Po Valley around 1400 B.C.

3. ITALY

The descendants of the Stone Age or Neolithic men in Italy are often referred to as the *Aborigines*. Some scholars identify them with the Ligurians. Who they were or what their language was related to we do not know. They were perhaps related to the primitive inhabitants of Greece, the Pelasgians, and we shall refer to them as being of the early Mediterranean stock and speaking a Mediterranean or Aegean tongue of which we can only postulate a few words. When the Latin tribes moved from the Po Valley before 1000 B.C., they fought their way to the Tiber River and settled along its banks, and to the south. This was a commanding location, particularly as there was only one ford across the Tiber at a place where later rose the city of Rome. Merchant traffic moving by land was bound to pass here and the Tiber gave a ready outlet to the sea. Not long after, Oscan and Umbrian contingents followed their Latin cousins farther south; but they were far greater in numbers and came in successive waves. According to some authorities a group of them known as the Siculi [3] entered first and were pushed down into the toe of the boot and into Sicily, which was to be named for them. The Oscans followed and settled throughout central and southern Italy; the Umbrians were considerably checked by the Ligurians and certain Pelasgian allies who had been driven by the Achaeans from Greece. The Umbrians and closely related tribes, the Sabines, Paeligni, Marsi, were pressed into the mountains of central Italy. Around 800 a horde of non-Indo-European folk from Lydia arrived by sea. These Etruscans settled an expanse of territory just north of the Tiber. During the Eighth century B.C., Sabine or Sabellian settlers began to come among the Latin towns and, although they tended to lose their Oscan speech, they secured such political control that later they formed the bulk of the patrician class among the Latins. In the Sixth century Etruria took possession of Latium and established a line of Etruscan kings; the last of these, Tarquinus Sextus, was driven out, with Sabine help, in 509. Hateful as this foreign rule was to the Latins, we must not forget that it was the Etruscans who really founded Rome. The city was just a little farming town on several of the ridges or hills

---

[3] Other scholars believe that the Siculi were of the aboriginal race.

overlooking the Tiber. The Tarquins surrounded it with walls and taught its rural inhabitants the value of city dwelling and certain institutions. The Romans learned fast. With the Tarquins once expelled they formed a defensive alliance with the Latin League (certain Latin towns to the south of them) in 493 and began to extend their conquests. This extension included the whole of Italy by 201 which marked the close of the Second Punic War.

4. LATIN LANGUAGE

It was the conquering of the Greek town of Tarentum, on the gulf which marks the instep of the " boot," that gave Rome her literature and incidentally the beginnings of a literary tongue. As we shall observe presently, Greek words had been seeping in among the lower-class Romans, particularly through Etruria; but the taking of Tarentum (272 B.C.) was Rome's first formal introduction to Greek culture. The soldiers carried back with them to Rome a Tarentine boy, Andronicus, who, shortly before 240, became the first Latin literary poet.[4] Previous to his time the Latins had learned to manipulate their language very well, in law codes and decrees; they even had popular poetry in a crude meter, the Saturnian; but all of this lacked refinement. We shall now list the successive stages of the Latin tongue:

(1) Primitive Latin: recorded only in a few inscriptions (:: — 240 B.C.)

(2) Early Latin: developed by such poets as Livius Andronicus, Naevius, Ennius, L. Pomponius, Pacuvius, and Accius, Plautus, Terence (240–90 B.C.)

(3) Latin of the Golden Age: under Lucretius, Catullus, Cicero, Caesar, Vergil, Horace, etc. (90 B.C.–14 A.D.)

(4) Silver Latin: a continuation of the style of such writers as Livy and Propertius (14 A.D.–160)

(5) Archaizing, but late, Latin (160 A.D.–395)

(6) Early Medieval Latin (395 A.D.–524)

(7) Low Latin (524 A.D.–790)

(8) Middle Latin (790–the Renaissance)

(9) Modern Latin (Renaissance–)

Ennius was the outstanding figure in the second period. In his

---

[4] He was commonly known as Livius Andronicus because he was first a slave in the Livy family.

Annales (189–169) he created the Latin hexameter after the Greek model; he began the writing of double consonants where so pronounced; he improved the notation of vowel sounds. Rhetoric reached a very high and, shall we say, artificial point in the Golden Age; in the Silver period, which we close with the death of Suetonius (160 A.D.), epigrammatic unperiodic sentences were the rule. Archaizing Latin, where the great models of the Golden era were rather slavishly imitated, is here indicated as ended with the death of Ausonius (395). There were some distinguished writers in the next period, such as Boethius (d. 524), but the invasions were inciting men to look towards the new. The closing of all the schools, save the cathedral and the monastic, in 529, by decree of Justinian, did not much affect Gaul (which had succumbed to the Franks in 492) but it deprived all of Latindom of its centers for pagan Latin culture.

5. GRADUAL EVOLUTION FROM INDO-EUROPEAN

Having defined conditions in Italy and among the primitive Indo-Europeans, we can best show the genius of the Latin language by a brief sketch of how it slowly evolved itself. Turning again to the diagram on page 3, the student will observe that the Latins traveled in successive stages with other groups before they reached the Tiber alone. We postulate Stage I as the period when the western Indo-European tribes were together; Stage II after the Germans and Italo-Celts had moved off; Stage III when the Germans had been left by the way; in Stage IV the Latins still formed a unit with the Osco-Umbrians; in Stage V the Latins had settled alone in Italy and were influenced casually by other peoples. Any attempt to speculate upon the duration in time of each of these stages is a guess; but from two to three hundred years is not an unlikely estimate. We shall sketch the linguistic progress achieved in each of these stages.

I. *The Indo-European tongue.* — Indo-European was a very flexible tongue: the vowels were seldom stable — *e* and *o* could alternate — a vowel was sometimes lengthened, sometimes reduced to nothing, or to an indeterminate sound. The nouns, verbs, pronouns, and adjectives were so highly inflected that each word was an independent element in itself. These inflected forms had a dual (denoting two) as well as a singular and a plural.

Nouns had a declension distinction between animate and inanimate (neuter) objects. There were eight cases to the declensions: nom., acc., gen., dat., abl., loc., instrumental, voc.

Verbs (some ending in vowel and some not) possessed a highly developed system for indicating the aspect or manner of an action; little attention was paid to tense or time. A subjunctive in *-e* or *-o* was formed to indicate " expectation " in an action, an optative mode in *-ye* denoted a possible action or a wish. The simple affirmation, which we call indicative, could be shaded in many ways: causative action, intensive, iterative aspect; but chiefly the speaker was concerned with whether the affirmed action was completed or incomplete. The imperfective and perfective forms of the indicative, which expressed this distinction, were certainly the commonest on the lips of the Indo-European speaker. For these he had endings both active and middle, to indicate whether the action was brought to bear upon the subject, or upon something else; e.g., I beat myself (middle voice) or I beat some one else (active voice). In the imperfective aspect both the middle and the active voice had two sets of endings apiece, today called primary and secondary, which was the only way in which the Indo-European speaker could suggest present or past action. Some imperfective verbs also had a variant stem, an aorist with secondary endings only; this stem expressed the action in its simplest form, with no concept of duration. The Indo-European verb probably indicated an impersonal form by the addition of a suffix *-r*.

Adjectives had at least two distinct series of endings for two grammatical categories of nouns (which were later designated as masculine and feminine); the syntactical difference between these two sets of nouns was very real but the reason is obscure to us (there was at first no idea of sex).

Indo-European had certain invariable particles which were placed in apposition to inflected forms to strengthen or shade the meaning slightly. These invariables (sometimes stereotyped nouns) did not govern anything; they were always in apposition in Indo-European. They are the ancestors, however, of our prepositions, conjunctions, and adverbs.

Of the personal pronouns and indefinites, we shall say nothing except that they were highly inflected with endings slightly different from those of the nouns.

A distinguishing feature of Indo-European syntax was the use of verbal nouns and relative constructions.

II. *Germanic and Italo-Celtic groups together* (2000 B.C.) — The syntax and noun declensions remained much the same as in Stage I; but the verb showed some changes. The subjunctive and optative were fused and probably certain of the other modal aspects were lost or confused; but the imperfective and perfective distinction in the indicative was developing still further, now spreading to the subjunctive:

	Imperfective	*Perfective*
Indicative	Present	Present
Subjunctive	Present Past	Present

III. *Italic and Celtic peoples (after 2000 B.C.)* — Ablative and instrumental singular fell together; locative, dative, ablative, and instrumental of plural coincided.   Many new nouns were built with suffixes.   Certain changes in the declension endings — notably a borrowing of the adverbial ending –*i* for a genitive singular in place of –*os* — took place.   In the verb secondary and primary endings no longer had any suggestion of time.   The scheme of imperfective and perfective was enlarged still further:

	Imperfective	*Perfective*
Indicative	Present Future	Present Future
Subjunctive	Present Past	Present

The subjunctive was now being made with suffixed –*a* and –*s*, and perhaps with –f–.   From the subjunctive imperfective present was constituted a future.   The middle endings were confused in the third person with the impersonal ending –*r* which was now used as a passive.

IV. *The Italic Group (after 1400 B.C.)* — The flexible nature of the earlier speech was becoming impossible.   The old invariable words in apposition were now beginning to function as genuine prepositions, conjunctions, and adverbs.   The vowels were becoming more stable.   There were many shifts in consonant articulation; e.g.,

$$gh >[5] \qquad x \text{ (when initial } > h).$$
$$bh > \qquad f$$
$$dh > \qquad f$$
$$-tl- > \qquad -kl-$$
$$-n > \qquad -m$$

[5] The sign (>) is to be read "became" or "becomes."   When turned the other way (<) it means "from" or "derived from."

All final consonants were weakening. The type of the combined ablative-instrumental ending *-od* was spreading into other declensions as *-ad, -ed;* the genitive plural ending *-asom* was spreading from the pronouns through some of the noun declensions. The dual had now been lost. The imperfective-perfective scheme was still more developed in tenses:

	Imperfective	*Perfective*
Indicative	⎰Present ⎱Past Future	⎰Present ⎱Past Future
Subjunctive	⎰Present ⎱Past	Present

V. *Latin.* — The Latins (c. 1000 B.C.) descended further into Italy and their language continued to develop radically, but now, of course, independently of the Oscan and Umbrian peoples.

-s-(between vowels) had been pronounced like *z;* between 450–350 B.C. the Latin speakers changed it to *-r-;* this is called rhotacism; *meliosem > meliorem.*

d in certain instances, became an *l;* e.g., *dacrima > lacrima.*

gi > i; mag + ior > maiior

di > i; e.g., *Diovis > Iovis*

y (between vowels) tended to disappear; e.g., **stayo > stao > sto*

Interior short vowels (not initial or final) tended to become either *i* or *u;* after *w, r, l, n, m* they most often disappeared; e.g., *surego > surgo, aeuitas > aetas,* but *oc-cano > occino, ac-capio > accipio, oc-capo > occupo.* Final long vowels tended to become short; final short vowels tended to disappear; e.g., *benē > benĕ, forīs > forĭs, etĕ > et, nequĕ > nec, seiuē > seu, utĭ > ut.*

A hard *l* (like the *l* in English *children* or *milk*) would often change a preceding *i* or *e* to an *o* or *u;* e.g., *velle* but *volo, familia* but *famulus.*

In the interior of a word an *r* not followed by another consonant would change any short vowel preceding it to an *e: im-paro > im-pero; separo* also becomes **sepero.*

Short vowels were well preserved in initial syllables.

Consonant groups tended to weaken; e.g. **torc-mentum* (< *tor-*

---

* An asterisk (*) indicates that the word must have existed, although it has not been seen in any text. It is postulated.

queo) > *tormentum*, *louksmen > *lumen*, *louksna > *luna*, *iouxmenta > *iumenta*.

By the third century the locative singular had disappeared; where it survived isolatedly as in *Romae, Tusculi, Karthagini*, it was confused with the genitive or dative. The ablative endings *–od*, *–ed, –ad* lost the *d*.

Logical and regular series of noun, verbal, and adverbial forms were developed by analogy; the imperfective and perfective forms were completed throughout and, with their new names, were:

	Imperfective	*Perfective*
Indicative	Present Imperfect Future	Perfect Pluperfect Future Perfect
Subjunctive	Present Imperfect	Perfect Pluperfect

Above all the Latin vocabulary became increased by many borrowings from the Greek, Mediterranean (Ligurian), Oscan, and Umbrian, and even from Etruscan and Phœnician. After the Latin League of 493 B.C. the city of Rome took unquestionable lead; her speech, the *urbanitas*, became the norm for good Latin. Certain rustic Latin words, however, continued to creep in. It was the Latin of Rome which determined to preserve the *h* which was silent in the country before Cicero's time, as well as the final *s* which the rustics wanted to drop. Not even those who dwelled in Rome were able to preserve final *m*, which was very weak indeed. The rustics also pronounced *ae* as *e* and *au* as *o*. But Rome could not hold out against these normal changes forever; they were in the " drift " of the language and the people.[6]

6. GRAMMAR AND DRIFT

Not long after a language begins to be a medium for literature there always comes grammar. The new poetry, or prose, which pleases the public best is considered a model to be copied, and the words, inflections, and sentence structure employed by the exemplary author are analyzed, classified, and definitely adopted as a norm or set of rules for all who would speak and write to advantage. This advent of grammar immediately slows down the process of

[6] See Marouzeau in the MSLP, XVII, 266–80.

language change. The drift continues among the vulgar folk, but their changing speech is called barbarism and solecism, until they also tend to be conservative and adhere to grammar whenever they can. But the drift — that line of least resistance which the unhampered speaker of the language wishes to follow — is ever at hand. Let the schools once relax their grasp upon the people and then the speech moves on.

Indo-European had no written literature, so far as we know, and consequently it had no grammar rules to slow up its drift into Latin and other dialects. But once a written Latin literature came into existence, there was a continual struggle between drift and grammar, from 240 B.C. until the present day. For example, the schools could restore a final –s which the Latin speaker wished to drop; but the schools weakened or disappeared in the period 390–529 A.D. and Latindom immediately drifted hopelessly into Vulgar Latin and Romance. The French language, in turn, came to be fixed by grammar in the seventeenth century, and the language has not been permitted to drift much since then. But whether the schools will again relax their vigilance is a question for the future, and we refer you to the last chapter of this book.

REFERENCES [6]

VENDRYES, J., *Le langage* (Paris; *La Renaissance du livre*, 1921).

SAPIR, EDWARD, *Language* (New York: Harcourt, Brace, 1921).

BLOOMFIELD, LEONARD, *Study of Language* (2nd ed., New York: Holt, 1933).

MEILLET ET COHEN, *Les langues du monde* (Paris: Champion, 1924).

MEILLET, A., *Introduction à l'étude comparative des langues indo-européennes* (7th ed., Paris: Hachette, 1934).

MEILLET, A., *Esquisse d'une histoire de la langue latine* (3rd ed., Paris: Hachette, 1933).

MAROUZEAU, J., *Le latin* (2nd ed., Paris: H. Didier, 1927).

JESPERSEN, K., *Language* (London: Allen and Unwin, 1922).

GRAFF, WILLEM L., *Language and Languages* (New York: Appleton, 1932).

KENT, ROLAND G., *The Sounds of Latin* (Language Monographs, No. 12, 1932).

STOLZ, F., and SCHMALTZ, Y., *Lateinische Grammatik* (5th ed., Munich: C. H. Beck, 1928).

BUCK, C. D., *Comparative Grammar of Greek and Latin* (2nd ed., Univ. of Chicago Press, Chicago, 1937).

[6] References in the earlier chapters are given in order of importance to the elementary student.

II

LATIN AND VULGAR LATIN

7. SPREAD

After the final expulsion of the Etruscan Tarquin in 509 B.C. the little town of Rome, much improved by the years of Etruscan domination, began to extend her influence. She was fortunately situated at the Tiber ford where two of the chief roads running north and south intersected. First Rome assumed a dominant position over the thirty odd Latin towns, her immediate neighbors; then she reached out further and took over the control of the rest of Italy which was Oscan in speech and tradition, finally including the Greek colonies on the southern coasts, the Etruscans to the immediate north of her, the Umbrians in the mountains to the northeast, and the Celtic tribes of Cisalpine Gaul in the extreme north. The Greek colonies of southern Italy were absorbed by the fall of Tarentum in 272. Rome was supreme in Italy after 270 B.C. except for occasional revolts. Latin literature, which began as an imitation of the Greek, was a direct result of this capture of Tarentum. The first piece of Latin literature was a translation of the *Odyssey* by Livius Andronicus, a young Greek captured at Tarentum. In 240 this same Romanized Greek introduced Latin plays after Greek models at the *ludi romani*.

8. NEW VOCABULARY

The immediate question now before us is one concerning the influence of Oscan, Greek, and Etruscan elements on the Latin vocabulary. As the newly conquered peoples came to adopt Latin for their daily use it is inconceivable that they did not retain some of their native expressions which rapidly passed into the lower-class speech of Rome. F. Lot has very aptly remarked that a bilingual people, when they become monolingual, as a last act flood into the victorious language what remains of the vocabulary of the disappearing speech. Words of Mediterranean origin which entered the Latin vocabulary were: *vinum* (wine), *rosa* (rose), *asinus* (ass), *miser* (wretched), *ficus* (fig), *lilium* (lily), and *funda* (sling). The Etruscans gave Latin such theatrical terms as *histrio* (actor), *subulo* (flute player), and *persona* (mask). It is very likely that they contributed also: *Roma, urbs* (city), *aerumna* (suffering), *fenestra* (hole in the wall), *forma* (form), *spurius* (illegitimate), *satelles* (bodyguard) and many other words not definitely traced as yet.

A distinction between Oscan and rustic Latin is often difficult to make. From one or the other of these are derived: *bos* (cow), *popina* (tavern), *anser* (goose), *ovis* (sheep), *infimus* (lowest), *sifilare* (whistle), *haedus* (kid), *aquila* (eagle), *mutilus* (without horns), *casa* (hut), *arbiter* (witness), etc. It must be remembered that we are here citing only those rustic expressions which were later admitted into the refined language of Rome, but there were doubtless many hundreds of such patois words which continued to be used by the common people of Italy and which have since disappeared, leaving no trace. It is possible to assume some phonetic influence from Oscan, such as the use of *u* for *o* and *i* for *e* in southern Italy, which has survived into the Romance dialects of that area.

After the fall of Tarentum and contact with the Greek cities of the south the Latin soldiers and common people adopted a host of Greek terms into their speech, of which some six hundred at least were later admitted into cultivated Latin. The serious writers of the period (250–100 B.C.) did not share this enthusiasm of the common herd for Hellenisms. Although Andronicus, Ennius, Plautus, and others were using Greek models, they scrupulously avoided padding the Latin language with Greek words and constructions; they even used *Camena* for *Musa!* It is true that Plautus sought to produce comic effects and in representing the " hoi polloi," he spattered Greek about more freely. Some of the Greek words which the plebians succeeded in forcing early upon the aristocratic opposition were: *colaphus* (blow with fist), *sumbolum* (sign), *camera* (vaulted roof), *spata* (sword), *spatula* (a broad piece), *massa* (mass), *talentum* (a sum of money), *macina* (device), *tecina* (trick), *caerefolium* (chervil, a salad herb), *oleum* (oil), *balineum*, (bath), and the verbal suffix *–issare* (< Greek ιζειν, pronounced [idzen]). Q. Ennius (239–169), with all his fondness for a pure Latin vocabulary, made a great innovation when he introduced the Greek hexameter metre into his *Annales* (189–169); previous to this date the Romans had been satisfied with a rough metre called the Saturnian. Ennius encouraged the use of double consonants, where appropriate, in the spelling of Latin. But it was not only Greek, Etruscan, and Oscan words that came into early Latin. The Phœnician merchants, or possibly the Carthaginians, contributed during this period (240–90 B.C.): *saccus* (sack), *mappa* (towel or napkin); and there came from the Celts of northern Italy such words as *carrus* (wagon), *carpentum* (two-wheeled cart), and *petorritum* (four-wheeled cart), terms of transport.

With the Golden Age of Latin literature (90 B.C. on) men of letters, such as Cicero, received their education partially in Athens, and in Rome at the hands of Greek slaves. It is no wonder that the barrier against Greek terms was lowered and many such words now entered. Cicero introduced *bibliotheca* (library) from the Greek βιβλιοθήκη, and he formed *qualitas* (quality or " which-ness ") on *qualis* (which), after the model of Greek ποιότης from ποῖος. Cicero also coined *medietas* (half), and Vergil devised the word *insomnium* (sleeplessness), but these were not from Greek models. Certain Latin words such as *ratio* (account), *puto* (calculate), and *ars* (art) received expansion of meaning from association with their Greek equivalents λόγος (reason), λογίζομαι (reflect), and τέχνη (trade). So frequent did a knowledge of Greek become that a hundred years after Cicero the Emperor Claudius advised a foreigner " cum utroque sermone nostro sit paratus."[1]

The Roman influence was extending beyond Italy. By 238 B.C. the Latins had gone into Sardinia; and as a result of the Punic Wars the Romans entered Spain in 200 B.C. and in 120 B.C. occupied the road across southern France into Spain. With the conquests of Cæsar (59–51 B.C.) the Latin language was carried still farther, throughout long-haired Gaul as far as the island of Britain. Cæsar was assassinated in 44 B.C. In 31 B.C. occurred the Battle of Actium which destroyed the pretensions of Mark Anthony and raised Octavian to power. Octavian received the title of Augustus in 27 B.C. and that same year he went into Gaul to organize it. Julius Cæsar had reduced the German tribes beyond the Gaulish border into some submission but they were not conquered. The Romans were forced to keep an army massed along the borders to hold them back, except for those individuals who entered peacefully. It is true that the Italians and Gauls enjoyed a considerable trade with the barbarian Germans during this era, and that many German troops began to swell the Roman armies.

New Celtic words entered Latindom through Gaul: *alauda* (lark), *arapennis* (half acre), *benna* (carriage), *bracae* (breeches), *caballus*

---

[1] "That he be furnished with both our languages." Suetonius, *Claud.*, 24.1.

(nag), *cerevisia* (beer), *leuca* (league), *saga* (coarse woolen blanket or mantle), etc. Josef Brüch has counted 102 German words which also entered common Latin at this time, before 402 A.D.: such as *alisna* (awl), *bakko* (swineflesh), *balk* (beam), *balla* (ball), *banda* (ribbon), *bank* (bench), *baro* (freeman), *bastjan* (build), *beber* (beaver), *binda* (bandage), *blank* (white), *blund* (blond), *bord* (side), *brakko* (dog), *brammon* (roar), *brand* (firebrand or sword), *brasa* (glowing coal), *brekan* (break), *brun* (brown), etc. We might say roughly that a Latin speaker in Italy during the Empire was apt to have some 1200 Greek words, some 100 Germanic, and 70 odd Celtic words in his vocabulary, as well as his native Latin roots.[2]

9. WHAT IS VULGAR LATIN?

This definition presents some difficulty, for present-day scholars are not entirely in accord on this matter. Perhaps a better way of approaching the subject would be to ask first what is Classical Latin. The view which has long found favor and which is still held by many scholars is as follows:

Vulgar Latin was the true speech of Rome and the rest of the Latin-speaking world. Beside it, Classical Latin was an artificial literary embellishment, owing a great deal to Greek teachers of grammar. Cicero delivered his orations in this literary tongue, but when he withdrew to his home, his speech represented a much freer usage. Vulgar Latin then had a continuous existence in Rome itself from Plautus to Charlemagne, independent of the language of literary tradition which we call classical.[3]

But the present writers prefer the following formulation, accepted and developed for the most part by linguistic scholars in France, for which we refer to certain articles and books by Ferdinand Lot, Marouzeau, Antoine Meillet, and Tenney Frank (see the end of the Introduction and the references at the end of this chapter). The variety of Latin spoken *naturally* at Rome began to be used for literature during the third and second centuries B.C. The immediate effect of this was to slow up somewhat the normal drift of the Roman speech, but no wide gap developed as yet between the speech of the people native to Rome and their literary medium — between the *urbanitas* and Classical Latin. It is reasonable to assume that

---

[2] This Celtic figure is based upon an actual count of the Celtic etymologies given in the Meillet etymological dictionary, *q.v.*

[3] For this view consult C. D. Buck, *op. cit.*, p. 27 ff.

during the second and first centuries B.C. the Classical idiom received rhetorical embellishments of rhythm and metaphor, as practiced by the oratorical schools of Rome and Athens, while the *urbanitas* retained the elements of familiar discourse such as affectionate diminutives; but still the educated natives of Rome spoke more or less as they read and wrote. Cicero refers to his own familiar use of Latin, meaning, of course, his use of endearments, lack of formal rhetoric and perhaps accepted items of current pronunciation such as *multu* for *multum*, used also by Vergil in the *Aeneid* (I, 3). It must be understood, of course, that there were native Romans in the lower classes who were not affected by any refinement of language. These people were apt to retain archaisms (expressions that had gone out of use), simplicity of sentence structure, and poverty of vocabulary. We admit the existence of such speakers as these but, unlike those who define Vulgar Latin differently, we do not believe that the influential classes of society spoke in such a loose and impoverished way. There were *graeculi* among the slaves and freedmen, and there were Oscan and Umbrian settlers; these, to be sure, misused the *urbanitas* shamefully.

After the reign of Augustus (31 B.C. to 14 A.D.) matters in Rome took on a different hue. The importance of the colonies became greater and greater. The old educated Roman families tended to disappear or sink into insignificance. Politicians or men of letters flocked to Rome from Spain, Gaul, and distant provinces. These newcomers wished to write with purity, but their daily speech was cast in a mold different from that which Vergil or Horace would have tolerated. Add to this the facts that many of the most unrefined elements of Roman society were acquiring wealth and importance, and that there began a wave of Syrian immigration into the western provinces.[4] Provincialisms in speech lost their stamp of shame, so that, beginning with the second century A.D., a distinct Vulgar Latin speech may be said to have existed beside the Silver Latin of literary tradition. By the time we reach the fifth century, it is probable that the two — the written Latin of tradition and the Vulgar Latin — had grown so far apart that the literary language required some form of interpretation to make it easily comprehended by the uneducated. Even some late grammarians, such as Virgilius Maro (sixth century A.D.), no longer understood the gender system of the classic texts. We must distinguish between these things: the *urbanitas* of the first century A.D., observed with care in

[4] Dill, *Roman Society in Gaul in the Merovingian Age* (London, 1926), p. 244.

the educated strata but tinged with vulgarisms more and more as one descended the social scale, and last of all a definitely constituted Vulgar Latin (which we would prefer to say assumed a more clearly defined shape after 100 A.D.) arising with the advent of social changes and their accompanying tolerance of vulgarisms in ever-increasing number.[5]

10. CHARACTERISTICS

With these definitions in mind, let us examine the sources of our knowledge of Vulgar Latin:

(1) Good writers who intentionally introduced vulgarisms for effect, just as we use slang. Horace wrote *auricula* for *auris* (Satire IX); Petronius used vulgarisms throughout a whole episode of his *Satyricon;* namely, in the *Cena Trimalchionis.* Vergil used an occasional popular pronunciation to aid his metre: *multum* with silent final *m* (*Aeneid* I, 3), *Laviniaque* with *i* as a semiconsonant (*ibid.* I, 2), also in *abiete* (*ibid.* II, 16). Plautus's language is not precisely Vulgar Latin, as we have indicated above, but it is the Latin of Rome before the refined era of the first century B.C. and it shows popular tendencies.

(2) Writers who knew no better language; and here we must indicate different degrees of vulgarity. Some who sought to write were more ignorant than others. There are certain rhythmic formulas that have survived which represent a low type of Latin. However, most of the material in this class (2) is a shade better, such as the *Peregrinatio sanctae Aetheriae* (Spain or southern France *c.* 381) — a " Cook's Tour account " of the Biblical Lands — the *Mulomedicina* (*c.* 400), a treatise on veterinary medicine, and certain formulary documents of the Merovingian kings. Then there were writers whose best Latin was not so disreputable and among these we list Gregory of Tours with his *Historia Francorum* (*c.* 580), the *Italas Latina* (second century A.D.) and its descendant, the Vulgate Bible of Saint Jerome) (390–404 A.D.). Certain Latin versions of folkbooks pertaining to the Alexander legend, as the *Commonitorium Palladii* and the letters of Alexander, belong in this third group. All of the texts just mentioned are products of the later Empire. Earlier are the *Bellum Africanum* and the *Bellum Hispaniense,* accounts of Roman wars during the Republic, which contain a

[5] H. F. Muller and Pauline Taylor, *A Chrestomathy of Vulgar Latin,* stress the use of vulgarisms by the churchmen (p. 2 ff). However, such evidence must be used with caution; cf. M. B. Ogle, in *Language,* VIII, 237.

considerable number of unconsciously rustic forms. Of course even the most ignorant of these writers did not write exactly as he spoke; everyone had *some* learning, though it might be small. The truest picture of Vulgar Latin as it actually was spoken can be gained from sources (3), (4), and (5) to which we now proceed.

(3) Grammatical glosses in which a grammarian indicates expressions to be avoided by anyone who would wish to use literary Latin. Chief among these was the *Appendix Probi* (200–320 A.D.), compiled by a grammarian Probus, of Northern Africa or possibly teaching in Rome. This glossary lists two hundred and twenty-seven correct forms followed by the corresponding vulgarisms;

e.g., calida	non	calda	ostiae	non	hostiae	
cochlea	non	coclia	vapulo	non	baplo	
globus	non	glomus	vobiscum	non	voscum	
apes	non	apis	pridem	non	pride	
exter	non	extraneus	adhuc	non	aduc	etc.

Then there are the grammatical writings of Quintilian and Aulus Gellius, as well as many anonymous glossators (see the *Corpus Glossariorum Latinorum* commonly abbreviated as CGL).

(4) Latin inscriptions, unearthed by the archæologists. A marvelous collection of these is in the vast *Corpus Inscriptionum Latinarum* (abbreviated as CIL). We add a few inscriptions from those discovered at Pompei:

1. Otiosis locus hic non est, discede morator (CIL. IV. 813)
2. Secundus pedicavd [6] pueros. . . (*Ibid.* 2048)
3. Quid pote tan durum saxso aut quid mollius unda ? dura tamen molli saxsa cavantur aqua (*Ibid.* 1895) [7]

Translation: 1. " This is no place for loafers. Get away, idler." 2. " Secundus has trapped youths." 3. " What can be so hard as a rock, or what more soft than a wave ? And yet hard rocks are hollowed out by soft water."

(5) Reconstruction from the later Romance languages — the descendants of Vulgar Latin.

(6) Vulgar Latin words which have been carried over into non-Romance tongues such as Germanic languages, Arabic, Judæo-Romance, and Celtic (c. 400 A.D.).

---

[6] *pedicavd* for *pedicavit.*
[7] *pote* for *potest; tan* for *tam; saxso* (indicating a pronunciation *sasso ?*) for *saxo.*

10 A. VULGAR LATIN AND *URBANITAS* OF ROME COMPARED

In numerous instances Vulgar Latin continued a drift which was present in early Latin, but which had been retarded for centuries by grammar influence on the daily speech.

We shall now give in outline form the main particulars in which the Vulgar or provincial speech of the Empire (250–500 A.D.) differed from the *urbanitas* of Rome (during its best period):

A. Vocabulary (or Lexicography)

1. Words to which the *urbanitas* or speech of Rome gave poetic extension of meaning usually kept their restricted sense in Vulgar Latin; e.g., *robur, virtus.*

2. Vulgar Latin often restricted the meaning further than should have been expected, with due attention to the historical meaning of the words: e.g., *necare* (to kill > to drown), *ingenium* (genius > trick).

3. Quite often Vulgar Latin sought to achieve a witty effect by using a base word, of low connotation, as a general term — thus extending its meaning: e.g., *casa, caballus, testa.* Often, too, the meaning of a word was extended for no reason apparent to us, or perhaps because the other special words had been dropped: *infans, prehendere.*

4. Many foreign and dialect words were current which the *urbanitas* did not admit: *battalia, drappus.*

5. A considerable number of terms of the old Latin stock, common in Classical Latin, were dropped in Vulgar Latin for special reasons. Rustic speech does not need many relation words — prepositions, adverbs and conjunctions; second, if two words of different meaning begin to resemble each other in sound the one less used tends to drop; third, archaic words which have run their course and are retained only for poetic reasons are lost in vulgar speech. The vulgar speaker cannot distinguish between synonyms. On the other hand, there were some expressions, found in early Latin, which the better Latin speakers had dropped but which were active among the vulgar: *sepero* for *separo, siem* for *sim.*

6. Word Formation. The Vulgar Latin speakers frequently felt an urge to strengthen or extend the usefulness of the words they had by a variety of suffixes and prefixes. The prepositions *ad-, con-, de-, dis-, ex-, in-, re-, per-, sub, super, contra-* were prefixed

to existing words very freely. As Nyrop has suggested, when a preposition tends to be dropped from the language as a preposition its usefulness as a prefix is impaired. It is then that an additional prefix must be added; hence such a double prefix formation as *deexcitare*. The number of suffixes added to nouns and adjectives to denote degree of quality, noun of agent, etc., were many and they were employed very freely. Verbs also received suffixes but usually of two distinct types: (a) to denote the aspect or manner of the action, a distinction which later meant nothing at all as *–iscere, –icare*, or the type *perfect participle* plus *–are* (frequentative); (b) to form a verb from a noun or adjective — a denominative verb. Of type (a) the practice of taking the perfect participle of a verb difficult to conjugate and by adding *–are* putting the verb into the first conjugation became a common one indeed. The old frequentative idea was completely lost: *oblit are* (< *obliviscor*), *us-are* (< *utor*), *aus-are* (< *audeo*, doubtless *audeo* was often confused with *audio*). Last of all let us mention under word derivation the frequent practice of using a diminutive ending for endearment. Vulgar speech can never have enough of this practice. The Romance languages bear constant evidence of the fondness of Vulgar Latin speakers for hypochorisms in *–ellus, –itta, –icus, –ulus*.

Some new formations were also made in Vulgar Latin by imitating the sound an object makes: *tokk* (the sound of an object striking another), *tumbare* (the plunk made by an object falling into the hand). Such new formations are called *onomatopœias*.

B. Phonology (or Changes in Pronunciation).

1. Vowels

Latin ĭ	Vulgar Latin ē:	*minus* > *menus*
ŭ	ō	*sub* > *sob*
æ	ĕ	*lœtus* > *letus*
œ	ē	*pœna* > *pena*

By 400 A.D. (perhaps starting *c.* 200 A.D.) an immense change had taken place in the way words were accented. In the Latin of the Republic and early Empire there was a musical pitch to the words in a sentence. Emphasis of a sort was secured by raising the tone slightly. A Latin phrase of this earlier period was a musical line of steady intensity with higher notes for the important syllables. Suddenly, perhaps through imitation of dancing or marching rhythms

the speakers began to use an accent of stress or varying intensity.[8] Some foreign influence may have helped here. The immediate result was that unaccented vowels, except when initial or final — important positions — began again to be crowded out, to be dropped; e.g., *rotulum > rotlum, camera > camra, capitanus > captanus*. We express this usually by the statement that unaccented vowels in the intertonic and penult syllables began to drop after 200 A.D. They dropped more easily between certain consonants. This progressive tendency continued till about 700 A.D.; after that date there were no vowels left in these positions save those that could not be dispensed with because of adjacent consonants difficult to pronounce without them. The distinction between *long* and *short* vowels was merged into a distinction between *closed* and *open* vowels by 400 A.D.

An unaccented *au* in the initial syllable tended to become *a* when accented *u* followed in the next syllable: *augustus > agustus*.

II. Consonants.

a. An unaccented *i* or *e* before a vowel became *y* in pronunciation, as was the case with *g* before *e* or *i;* also with *gi̯, di̯: gentis >* **yentis, diurnus > *yornus, vestigia > *vesteya*.

b. *c* before *e* or *i* became *cy* (in Republic times) then became *ty* or *dy* (between two vowels). Later in Romance it had further changes; e.g., *centum > *tyentu, vicinus > *vidyinus*.

c. Final *m* in noun and verb endings was lost: *terram > terra, vendam > venda*.

d. The *v* or consonantal *u* lost its pronunciation equivalent to our English *w* and became similar to our English *v*, during the first century of the Empire.

e. *h* was silent in all positions save in German words; e.g., Lat. *homo > omo* but *h* in *honte* < German *haunitha* remains without change.

f. *qu* began to lose the *u* or labial element and to be pronounced like a simple *k*, particularly before *o* and *u: quomodo > komo'o*.

g. It is very probable that *t, p,* and *c* (before *a, o, u*) between two vowels began to weaken, in Gaul at least, to *d, b, g* respectively. The *b* and *v* between vowels had certainly weakened to a sound similar to the modern Spanish pronunciation of *b* or *v*, a sound

---

[8] Here again we are in the midst of controversy. We are following the statement of the case as given by Meillet, Havet, and others. See the Nicolau reference at the end of the chapter. For R. G. Kent and others the Latin accent was primarily a stress accent from the beginning and the classical pitch was due to the influence of Greek masters. See R. G. Kent in *TAPA*, LIII, 63 ff., and Debrunner in *IF*, 311 ff.

which we call the bilabial spirant and represent by a Greek β: *virtutis > virtudis, ciconia > cigonia, avis > a$\beta$is.*

h. Certain adjacent consonants began to affect each other: *ct > it, gd > id, cr > ir, cl > l'*, in Gaul by 300 A.D. *pt > tt, ns > s, rs > ss.*

C. Noun and Verb Forms (or Morphology)

1. For various reasons the standard Latin cases were reduced as follows[9]:

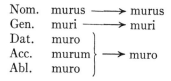

Nom. murus ⟶ murus
Gen. muri ⟶ muri
Dat. muro
Acc. murum ⟶ muro
Abl. muro

2. In northern Gaul the standard Latin verb tenses were considerably reduced in number in the Vulgar speech:

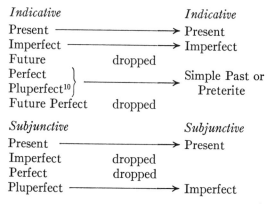

Indicative		*Indicative*
Present	⟶	Present
Imperfect	⟶	Imperfect
Future	dropped	
Perfect	⟶	Simple Past or
Pluperfect[10]		Preterite
Future Perfect	dropped	

Subjunctive		*Subjunctive*
Present	⟶	Present
Imperfect	dropped	
Perfect	dropped	
Pluperfect	⟶	Imperfect

3. Vulgar Latin also dropped the passive voice and substituted new passive forms such as **so amatus* (equals *sum amatus*), etc. Of the other verb forms Vulgar Latin kept the present infinitive, the present participle, and the perfect passive participle, this last as a simple past participle; e.g., *amare, amans, amatus.* The other participles and infinitives were lost. The gerund and the gerundive survived in a few instances as nouns: *vivenda* " food."

Late in the Vulgar Latin period, perhaps as late as the eighth

---

[9] With the loss of final *m* in vulgar Latin the dative, accusative, and ablative singular were virtually the same. The more simplified, analytic syntax of vulgar speech preferred prepositions plus one oblique case to a number of varied oblique cases without preposition.

[10] Survives as a Preterite only in the form *auret* "had" of the *Eulalia* poem (882 A.D.).

century, a new future tense became current. This was derived from the infinitive with the present indicative of the verb *habere: amare habeo* (pronounced *amar'aio*), " to love I have " which weakened to the meaning " I shall love."[11] Probably at the same time the past, or less vivid, future came into existence, developing from a combination of the infinitive with the imperfect indicative of *habere: amare habebam* (which was pronounced *amar'eba* or *amar'eβa*), " to love I had " equaling " I should love." These new constructions were used in all the persons and soon became the rule.

D. Syntax. In the *urbanitas* or best Latin of Rome, word order was a question of relative importance within a phrase. In Vulgar Latin the order *subject* and *predicate* and *complement* slowly began to predominate. This is the most natural word order for the human mind, once the pure mechanics of language have been made flexible and language is able to conform exactly to man's thought. Let us explain further. In our thought we normally begin with a concept, next we assert something about that concept, and finally we conclude with the manner, the time, or the result (object) of the assertion. If this thought order is translated immediately into words we have *subject + predicate + complement.* But language in its very beginning did not represent an orderly picture of man's thoughts: language began with rather complicated utterances expressive of emotion under certain circumstances. It is to the credit of the human mind that it gradually reduced and analyzed these complicated speech utterances during many centuries of improved thought until at last language order tended to coincide with the normal order of concepts. Those who are familiar with Greek will recognize that this ideal word order began to prevail there at an earlier period than it did in Latin.

As we should expect in any colloquial speech, Vulgar Latin shows a considerable poverty in the variety of constructions; there is a tendency to reproduce the thought as simply as possible, often with a disregard for logic and proper indication of antecedents.

Such in brief is a description of the Latin Vulgar speech in the period 100–700 A.D. The *urbanitas*, in its Silver Latin form, was still written by the elite but Rome followed the provinces and rustic Italy in tolerating a baser form of daily speech.

[11] Language does not need a future tense. This tense always develops later from the weakening of a desiderative or of an expression of necessity. Compare English *I shall go.* The so-called future of standard Latin was a weakened subjunctive (§ 5 III).

11. TRANSLATION EXERCISE

We shall close each chapter of this book with an artificial effort which may provoke criticism from scholars but which should prove a blessing for the beginner. We have chosen a passage from the *Satyricon* (CXV) of Petronius, a novel written mostly in good Silver Latin of Nero's court. We now begin by turning this into Vulgar Latin of the year 400 (as we reconstruct it) and at the conclusion of each chapter hereafter we shall revise this selection to illustrate the language changes discussed in the chapter. Here are the original and the first Vulgar Latin stages.

Petronius' Original. — Audimus murmur insolitum et sub diaeta magistri quasi cupientis exire belvae gemitum. Persecuti igitur sonum invenimus Eumolpum sedentem membranaeque ingenti versus ingerentem. Mirati ergo quod illi vacaret in vicinia mortis poema facere extrahimus clamantem iubemusque bonam habere mentem. At ille interpellatus excanduit et: Sinite me, inquit, sententiam explere; laborat carmen in fine. Inicio ego phrenetico manum, iubeoque Gitona accedere et in terram trahere poetam mugientem.

Reconstructed Vulgar Latin of 400 A.D., *indicating pronunciation changes.* — Audímus rúy(i) to eśtranyo de sotto (subtus) camre mayéstri kómo'o rúy(i)tus de una béstia qui volit eśire. Sequentes tonc sono trobamus Eumolpo sedente ante uno pergamíno mayno escriβente versos. Mirádi (< *mirati*) per oc kod elli lécuisset poema fac(e)re, ellā morte appressā, tiramus esso (< *ĭpsum*) clamante et commandamus elli venire ad racione. Sed elli torbatus entraβit en ira grande ed diśit: " Laśade mi mea sentencia complire; fines carm(i)nes est acra." Yo figo mano ad ello rabyoso et commando ad yidona venire ed tráy(e)re poéta ruyénte a terra.

Note that *x* is similar to English *sh* which we spell here *ś*. Observe the dropping of interior unaccented vowels. *Volit* has replaced *vŭlt*. The ablative absolute is still present with *ella morte appressa*. Above all observe that the vocabulary is not so varied. (The average college student in America today uses less than 60 per cent of the words found in standard literary English.) The conjunction *et* conforms in its final *t* to the sound which follows. *e* and *i* in hiatus are *y;* e(g)ó > yo. We have indicated the stress accent for certain of the words. The *–ci–* as in *racione* or *sentencia* < *sententia* indicates a pronunciation *ts;* here we have retained the late Latin spelling.

REFERENCES

LOT, F., in *Arch. Latin. Med. Aev.* VI, 97–159.

ERNOUT, A., and MEILLET, A., *Dictionnaire étymologique de la langue latine* (Paris: Klincksieck, 1932).[12]

GRANDGENT, C. H., *An Introduction to Vulgar Latin* (Boston: Heah, 1907).

MULLER, H. F., and TAYLOR, PAULINE, *A Chrestomathy of Vulgar Latin* (Boston: Heath, 1932).

BRÜCH, JOSEF, *Der Einfluss der Germanischen Sprachen auf das Vulgär-latein* (Heidelberg: Winter, 1913).

RICHTER, ELISE, *Beiträge zur Geschichte der Romanismen* (Halle: Niemeyer, 1934).

FRANK, TENNEY, *Economic History of Rome* (2nd ed., Baltimore: Johns Hopkins Pr., 1927), and in *Amer. Hist. Rev.*, XXI, 690.

NICOLAU, M. G., *L'origine du " cursus " rythmique et les débuts de l'accent d'intensité en Latin* (Paris: Soc. d'éd. " Belles Lettres ", 1930).

[12] A new edition of this is in preparation.

III

LOW ROMANCE (OR PRE-LITERARY FRENCH)

(700–1000 A.D.)

12. DEFINITION

It is during this period that the Latin speech suffered the greatest change, resulting in what we call Old French. It is a question of when and how grammatical influence became practically *nil* over the speech of the people, allowing the normal drift to make extraordinary headway. There were probably signs of this after 600 in Gaul, but it was the renaissance of Classical Latin studies begun by Charlemagne (ruled 768–814) in 780 that removed every trace of prestige from the Vulgar Latin of the people and transferred it to an artificial imitation of Cicero and Vergil to be taught henceforth in monastic and cathedral schools. Once the schoolmasters declared that the spoken Vulgar Latin was not Latin — in terms of Cicero — that it was *romanica* or Romance, a debased speech, the people ceased to observe rules of grammar.[1] The grammatically minded individuals reserved their efforts for the artificial language of the schools which we call today Middle or Medieval Latin. We distinguish these two: Vulgar from Medieval Latin, the former exclusively spoken, the latter written and spoken artificially by the schoolmen.

13. CHARLEMAGNE'S RENAISSANCE

Charlemagne studied Latin grammar with Peter of Pisa as early as 774; he continued under Paulinus of Aquilea in 776. We must remember that the emperor was a native German speaker and did not know the rustic Latin of Gaul except as a foreign language. Charlemagne was depressed by the state of the Latin used in the church. The mass was being corrupted daily by the ignorant clergy and the Bible MSS. and the writings of the Church Fathers,

[1] Meillet in *Bull. Soc. Ling. Paris*, XXXIV, xxv–xxvi.

because of many vulgar errors by copyists, were fast becoming unintelligible to some of the churchmen. After 780 Charlemagne sent letters to his abbots and bishops demanding a reform in ecclesiastical learning. Paulus Diaconus of Lombardy came to the emperor in 781 and in that same year Alcuin was summoned from the monastery of Yarrow in England to take charge of the court school. Alcuin was constantly at the court from 786 till 798, when he retired to his new abbey of Saint Martin's at Tours. For the efficiency of this renaissance we must thank Alcuin. England and Ireland were the two lands which had alone preserved a Latin worthy of the name, because there was no possibility of confusion there with the vernacular.

At the close of the century there came to Charlemagne's court Theodulphus, a Spanish Goth, and two Irish scholars, Clement and Joseph. Gradually this reform spread beyond its first limitations. Not only the Church but also the chancellors and those who studied the profane authors came to profit by the revived grammatical Latin. From the Rhine to the Loire, and including northern Burgundy, Charlemagne's immediate subjects began to transcribe the ancient authors with remarkable purity and correctness. The scribes of Saint Martin's at Tours continued a movement which had made but little headway hitherto, although it had begun during the reign of Charlemagne's father, Pepin. This was a reform of the writing hands. The old Merovingian MS. hand resembled nothing so much as a series of hen tracks. By forming the letters more carefully and by introducing capital letters from the rounded semi-uncial hand, in vogue in England and Ireland, the scriptorium of Tours developed what we call the Carolingian hand. This method of writing has never been surpassed. Later centuries debased it into the so-called Gothic or black-letter hand, but Italian scribes revived it in its earlier form and it is now the lower-case Roman alphabet which we find in modern books.

Charlemagne had a grammar of the German language compiled, but this has been lost. It was the first grammar of a spoken tongue to be composed since the days of Rome. As a Christmas present, in 801, Alcuin sent Charlemagne a copy of the Vulgate Latin Bible purged of its vulgarisms and errors. Most of the clergy were now capable of writing correct Latin verse. The only influence of this reform felt by the laity — the people at large — was that certain of their low Romance words which were associated with the church were checked a bit in their " drift " development. As already stated, the remainder of the Romance vocabulary hastened on its way to the Old French stage. Words that were thus partially checked by church influence are designated by us as semilearned. Here are a few: *siècle, livre, église, second.* If these same words had continued their strictly popular development we should say today **sille, *loivre, *cloise* or **claise, *sond* (*< *seont*).

The schools of Charlemagne continued in operation fairly well till after the death of his grandson, Charles the Bald, in 877. At that time learning became more restricted, withdrawing into certain monasteries and ecclesiastical centers such as Rheims and Chartres, but it was never lost entirely. The pronunciation of Classical Latin once more became slightly corrupted, but the divorce between Romance and Latin was complete.

13 B.   WRITTEN MATERIAL

Even fewer written texts are at hand to give an adequate picture of the low Romance speech than was the case with Vulgar Latin (see § 10 above). The common people did not write. The few texts that we do possess have distorted spellings: these are the Oaths of Strasbourg (842), the sequence, or hymn, of *Saint Eulalia* (882), the *Life of Saint Leger* (tenth century), the *Passion* (tenth century), the fragment of a sermon on *Jonah* (c. 1000), and a few glosses. This means that nearly all our knowledge of low Romance is based upon postulated or starred forms.

The Oaths of Strasbourg are frequently given much attention. Two grandsons of Charlemagne, Charles the Bald and Louis, formed a coalition against their brother Lothair. Charles swore his oath in German while his men swore in their native tongue — Romance. Louis reciprocated in Romance and his people in German. A chronicler, Nithard, has preserved these oaths, with a highly Latinized spelling in the case of the Romance versions. Here is the oath taken by Louis:

Pro Deo amur et pro christian poblo et nostro commun salvament, d'ist di en avant, in quant Deus savir et podir me dunat, si salvarai eo cist meon fradre Karlo, et in aiudha et in cadhuna cosa, si cum om pro dreit son fradra salvar dift, in o quid il mialtre si fazet. Et ab Ludher nul plaid numquam prindrai qui meon vol cist meon fradre Karle in damno sit.

14. FOREIGN INFLUENCES ON LOW ROMANCE

The Salian Franks who invaded northern Gaul under Clovis in 486 were too few in number,[2] to add much to the Gaulish Latin speech, although they secured political domination of the country. But the hordes of Rhine Franks who were gradually pushing peacefully over into eastern Gaul, colonizing Austrasia (modern Champagne and Lorraine), brought an enormous influence to bear, even upon the Latin speakers in Neustria, the adjacent territory to the west. Dagobert I was king of all Franks in 628. Pepin of Heristal, duke of Austrasia, overcame the Neustrians at the Battle of Testry in 687, and from then on Austrasia was definitely the leading state in Gaul. The Merovingian kings of Austrasia became weak: the last of them, Childerich III, was dethroned in 751 by Pepin, the father of Charlemagne. German was spoken as a second tongue, even in Neustria, by public officials as late as 850. At least we should judge this from the fact that Lupus of Ferrières sent his nephew and two other young nobles to Prüm in 844 to learn the German language (Letter XXXV). If an official of Neustria needed German it was because many of those with whom he came in contact spoke it. We might say that German disappeared as a spoken language in western Austrasia and in Neustria completely during the tenth century.[3] There was no Celtic spoken in Gaul after the fifth century, except perhaps in some of the remote mountainous districts of the south.[4]

To the 102 Germanic words introduced into Vulgar Latin before the year 400, the speakers of low Romance in Gaul added some 1,000, at least 16 per cent of their total vocabulary. North of the Somme River 70 per cent of the place names are Germanic; around Paris 50 per cent are German. South of the Loire the proportion is almost negligible. The common German words that were adopted fell into well-defined types (we give only one example of each, in parentheses): economic life (*waidanjan* > *gagner*), dwellings (*haim +* *ellu* > *hameau*), property (*allodis* > *alleu*), building (*bastjan* > *bastir*), personal toilette (*waskon* > *gascher*), war terms (*halsberga* > *hauberc*), housewifely duties (*wipan* > *guiper*), ornaments (*nuska* > *nosche*),

---

[2] They numbered only about a hundred thousand, while there were nearly two million Gallo-Latins.

[3] Richer of Rheims knew a few German words as shown in his *Historia* (991–998), § 69.

[4] Sidonius Apollinaris registers its disappearance among the Arverni. MGH. *Auct. Antiq.* VIII, XLI. 15–16.

expressions of character (*urguol* > *orgueil*), colors (*waisdo* > *guède*). Note that these types are words that pertain to the upper dominating class. Celtic was dead before the passing of Vulgar Latin into Romance but many Celtic words had remained in the Latin dialects of the people. Low Romance dignified the use of these while Vulgar Latin did not. We have recorded sixty-eight or more Celtic words in standard Latin; not all of these came down into Romance. Such words as *atinia* " elm," *bardus* " bard," and *belinuntia* "Apollinaris," did not survive among the people. Vulgar speech in Gaul used many others, however, so that we note at least 361 words of Gaulish provenance in French and Provençal. These Celtic words fell into more homely types than was the case with the borrowings from German: agriculture — 77 (e.g., *amblais* < **ambilatium*), household effects — 33 (*bache* < **bacca*), animals — 30 (*seus* < *segusius*), food and drink — 29 (*dousse* < *dolsa, drasche* < *drasica*), trees — 24 (*if* < **ivo*), plants — 18 (*breuil* < *brogilos*), body — 17 (*dor* < *durnu*), dress — 15 (*gonne* < **guna*), construction — 15 (*bief* < *bedo*), birds — 13 (*mauvis* < **melvi*), fish — 6 (*dars* < **darsus*), insects — 5 (*besaine* < **besena*), nontechnical words not easily classified — 40 (*pièce* < **pettia*), and the remainder divided among weapons, religion, literature, music, persons, sickness, and minerals. It is evident that the peasants were the last to hold to their Celtic.[5]

German contributed several prefixes and suffixes to Gaulish Romance: *for-* (*forchasser*) but usually appearing as *fre-* (*fredaine*); *misso-* (*mésalliance*); *-ing* (*esterlinc*); *-ward* (*cou–art*); and possibly *-in* (*wald* + *in* > O French *gaudine*). Celtic, on the other hand, gave French its system of counting by " twenties " where we should expect " tens " (*quatre-vingts, quinze vingts, onze vingts*); also an *-it-* combination for Latin *-ct-* (Lat. *noctem* > French *nuit*), and possibly the French pronunciation of *u*.[6]

In syntax or sentence structure Celtic influence is limited to only one possibility: the periphrasis of the type *C'est moi qui le fais* resembles very strikingly what we find in Celtic. The Germanic influence on Low Romance syntax was very strong. The constant

---

[5] This count of the Celtic element was made by Leslie Moss at the University of North Carolina. Her decision as to the Celtic nature of a word was based upon unanimity of agreement among the best lexicographers. In addition to the 361 words thus listed she noted 67 others where the authorities do not agree, which might be Celtic in source. If these are included we have a grand total of 428. The French grammarians do not admit usually more than a hundred Celtic words in French. Their count *must* be too low.

[6] It is possible that the extension of *apud* with the meaning " with " in Gallo-Latin was also due to Celtic influence.

use of *si* in Old French where the Old High German used *so* or *thanne* is one instance; still another is the completion of the meaning of a verb with an adverb, as in *lever sus, aler avec, traire avant*, for which compare modern English *raise up, go along, draw forward*. German made constant use of the idiom " man says " for " it is said," or " man went " for " they went "; surely this survives in the construction with the indefinite *on* in French. There were other cases of influence which would not be fully appreciated save by one who knows Old French well.[7]

After 827 the descent of the Norsemen on the coasts of France became serious. These hardy pirates came in long ships from Norway, and also from Denmark; they landed at river mouths, unloaded horses, and pillaged all they could find, before defense was organized. Charles the Bald treated with them more than once; finally in 886 they besieged Paris unsuccessfully. Charles the Simple, grandson of Charles the Bald, abandoned the territory which is now called Normandy to these Norsemen in 911. They became Christian in name and the sporadic invasions ended; but it was not till about 940 that they ceased to be offensive to the French. Their influence upon the language of the French was a contribution of more than ninety words, some of them surviving only in the Norman French dialects. They can be classified as maritime and fishing terms (*sigla* > *sigle*), features of the terrain (*haugr* > *hougue* " hill "), and a few isolated words not easily classified: *hora* > *hore* " little girl," *timbr* " forty skins " > *timbre* " martin skin," *tundr* > *tondre* " tinder." [7a]

15. ROMANCE PHONOLOGY

In the preceding sections we have examined the foreign influences which the Gallo-Roman speech had to meet as it obeyed its normal drift towards Old French (after 1000). These influences were the semilearned checking of a few words by the Latin-speaking schoolmen and the contributions of Celt, German, and Norseman. It remains to examine the changes led by the " drift " in transforming Vulgar Latin into Old French, during the so-called Low Romance period. Some of these alterations were under way in late Vulgar Latin, but we shall lump these with the rest in the interest of unity.

---

[7] Consult Holmes in *Language*, VII, 194–199 and *ibid.*, IX, 162.

[7a] Georgia Brewer checked these Norse borrowings in the standard etymological dictionaries. She found twenty-five surviving in Norman dialect and twenty-seven in Old French only. This leaves about thirty-eight in standard modern French.

For examples in English of how an accented vowel can spread or break, examine the English words *no*, *met*, and our pronunciation of Latin *me*. The vowel in *no* is not *ō* but *ō-ū*. The word *met* is pronounced in some parts of the southern United States as *mē-ĕt;* Latin *mē* becomes *mē-ĭ* on our tongues. This is precisely what happened, only more seriously, to Vulgar Latin accented vowels during the Low Romance period; but the accented vowel was not usually altered if a consonant followed it in the same syllable; e.g., the vowels in *ter-ra*, *car-ta*, *pon-tem* tended not to change, but in *pa-trem*, *ca-nis*, the accented vowel is **free** and not **checked** by an end consonant in the syllable.

A source of confusion, during Low Romance, was the group of vowels and consonants pronounced high in the front of the mouth. Such sounds are usually called palatals and the common ones are *i*, *y* (which we write *i̯* hereafter), *c*, *g*, *ch*, *ri̯*, *si̯*, *ti̯*, *ci̯*, *li̯*, *ni̯*, *mi̯*, and all other consonants followed immediately by a *i̯* (or *y*). These palatals corrupt or alter the pronunciation of adjacent sounds: compare English *Dontcha know* for *Don't you know* in which the *y* is the offending palatal.

Sometimes an intervening consonant disappears early in the course of change from Vulgar Latin to Old French, or it disengages a semi-vowel from itself; e.g., *nocte* > **noi̯te*, *habuit* > **a-u̯it*. When this semivowel, either *i̯* or *u̯*, becomes adjacent to the preceding vowel it usually forms a diphthong with it. In the following pages we shall call this disengaged semivowel " an epenthetic *i* or *u*." The adjective *epenthetic* may be used more generally to designate any sound inserted into the interior of a word, especially if it adds a syllable, but our use of the word will be specific, applying as we have indicated.

Vulgar Latin acquired a strong stress accent that tended to force out unaccented syllables within the interior of a word: *bònitátem* > *bontáde*, *cólapus* > *cólpus*. In most cases this dropping had already occurred before the Low Romance period, so we say that the *o* in *col-pus* developed as a checked *o* in Low Romance (although it was not checked in Latin). The *o* in *bontade* we should refer to as a checked *o* in an initial unaccented syllable. The lost *i* in *bontade* was in an intertonic syllable (between the main accent ′ and the secondary accent ˋ); the lost *a* in *colpus* was an unaccented penult vowel; the final *u* in *colpus* is called a final *u* because it is in the final syllable — even though it is not the last element in the word.

Having discharged ourselves of these preliminaries, we give in briefest form possible the table of the " drift " which altered Vulgar Latin into Old French.

16. THE RULES OF " DRIFT "

A. Accented Vowels[8]

Normally, free accented *a* > *e*: *claru* > *cler*, *ma-tre* > *me-re;* but before an *n* or *m* the *a* > *ai*: *manu* > *main*. If the *a* was preceded by a palatal sound (see above) none of these changes happened; it became, instead, *ie*: *cane* > *chien*, *capu* > *chief*. When an epenthetic *i* developed after the *a* an *ai* was the result with no further change: *lacte* > *lait*, *habeo* > Vulgar Latin **aio* > *ai*, an epenthetic *u* caused a resulting combination *ou*: *fagu* > **fau* > *fou*. When the *a* was in a checked syllable it made no change under any conditions: *carru* > *char*, *canto* > *chant*, *pasta* > *paste*.

A free accented *ę* (as in English *met*) > *ie*: *sęde* > *siet;* this was also true before an *n* or *m*: *bęne* > *bien*.[9] This new *ie* plus an epenthetic *i* > **iei* and then simple *i*: *lęctu* > **lieit* > *lit*. When *ę* was in a checked syllable it remained unchanged, although when checked by an *n* or *m* it might sometimes resemble a nasal *a* in sound if not in spelling: *ferrum* > *fer*, *lentu* > *lent* or *lant*.

A free accented *ẹ* (pronounced like *a* in English *mate*) > *ei* in the Low Romance period: *me* > *mei;* if preceded by a palatal, however, this *ẹ* was raised to an *i*: *cepa* > *cive*. The *ẹ* was also changed to *i* when followed by an *i* in the final unaccented syllable: **presi* > *pris*. When checked the *ẹ* was unchanged: *sẹp-ia* > *seche*. Before *n* or *m*, *ẹ* > *ei* normally: *plẹnu* > *plein;* and with a preceding palatal the reaction was also what we should expect: *racẹmu* > *raisin*. An *ẹ* when checked by *n* or *m* was apt to be pronounced *an* although spelled *en*: *vendem-ia* > *vendenge*. Recall that Classical Latin *ĭ* > *ę* in Vulgar Latin, so that many of our cases of *ę* are former occurrences of *ĭ* in good Latin: *vĭa* > *vęa* > *veie*.

A free accented *ǫ* (like *o* in English *not*) > *ue*: *bove* > *buef;* this was also true before an *n* or *m*, but often the Romance speaker preferred a plain *o* in this circumstance: *homo* > *uem* or *om*. When the *ǫ* was followed by an epenthetic *i* the result was **uei* > *ui*:

---

[8] An open vowel is always designated by an *open* circle, now called a hook, placed underneath the vowel. A closed vowel is indicated by a *closed* circle, or a dot, placed underneath.

[9] Any vowel followed by an *n* or *m* in Old French was apt to have a slight nasalized twang; but this is to be assumed and not cited in each individual case.

nôcte *nueit > *nuit.*   Checked ǫ remained: *ponte* > *pont, porta* > *porte.*

An accented ǫ (like *o* in English *note*) > *ou*, whether free or checked: *gǫla* > *goule, rǫssu* > *rous.*[9a] (It is probable that the *ou* checked was pronounced *u*, despite the spelling *ou*, while in the free position the *ou* was pronounced as spelled.) Before a nasal consonant (*n* or *m*) the ǫ underwent no visible alteration: *poma* > *pome, sǫmma* > *sǫmma* > *some.* Classical Latin *u* had become ǫ in Vulgar Latin.

An *i̧* free or checked did not alter under regular conditions: *villa* > *vile, ripa* > *rive, pinu* > *pin.* A *u̧* free or checked got the mixed vowel pronunciation of *ü* so well known in modern French, but there was no visible alteration: *nu̧du* > *nut, flu̧men* > *flum.* The diphthong *au* changed to ǫ very late in the Low Romance period, after most of the other alterations of sounds had taken effect: *causa* > *chose.*

B. Unaccented Vowels

We have noted the various positions of an unaccented vowel in the word. In the penult position the Vulgar Latin stressed accent was too much for such a vowel and forced it out. In the intertonic and final position the unaccented vowel was also dropped, unless it was an *a*, or unless some vowel was required to make the word pronounceable, when an *e* sound was retained: *atramentu* > *arrement, entro* > *entre, pasta* > *paste, quadriforcu* > *cadrforc > *carrefour;* but *claritate* > *clartet, homo* > *om.*

In the initial unaccented position (as first syllable in *carbone*) the vowels *e̦, ę, i̧, u̧*[10] remained unchanged, whether free or checked: *pe̦sáre* > *peser, fęllone* > *felon, fu̧mare* > *fumer, privare* > *priver.* An *a* in this position was also unchanged except for *one case:* when free and preceded by a palatal it became *e* (not *ie* as in accented position), *caballu* > *cheval*, but *avaru* > *aver.* The *au* became *o*, except for one case already mentioned under Vulgar Latin (cf. p. 21). The Low Romance and Old French speakers were never certain how to spell unstressed *o* and *ou* sounds; they hesitated considerably. Initial unaccented ǫ, free or checked, and ǫ free, presumably were pronounced *u̧* in Low Romance but they could be spelled *u, o,* or *ou: botellu* > *budel, bodel,* or *boudel.* On the other hand a checked initial ǫ was spelled and pronounced ǫ: *portare* > *porter.*[11]

[9a] See § 29 for further development of the *ou*.
[10] But *u̧* was pronounced *ü*.
[11] See for sporadic development of such an *o*, Holmes in *Language*, XI, 231–7.

C. Consonants

The strongest position a consonant can hold in a word — that is, the position where it is seldom subject to alteration — is either the initial position or directly after another consonant with which it does not make intimate combination: in *porter* the *p* is initial and the *t* is just as strong, being supported by the *r*. On the other hand, in such a combination as *veclu* the *l* is not in a strong position because it unites intimately with the *c* to form a palatal *l*. In the initial or strong position the following consonants make no visible alteration: *b, d, f, l, m, n, p, r, t, v*. The consonant *c* is unaltered before an *o* or a *u* (*cųrtu > court*) but it becomes *ts* in sound (although still spelled *c*) before an *e* or *i:* (*cera > cire*). Before an *a* the *c > ch: case > chies, falcare > falchier*. A *g* remains before *o* and *u;* it was already a *i̯* in Vulgar Latin before *e* and *i;* before an *a* it shifts to a *i̯* during the Low Romance period: *gagate > ie̯i̯et*, and this initial *i̯-* was then pronounced like an English *j* (in *jade*). The other *i* in this word is still pronounced as *y* (in *yet*) because it is medial (see following). The Latin *h* became silent; but in words borrowed from the German it was pronounced: *hache* < German *hapja*, but *om* < Latin *homo*. Initial *qu-* gradually lost its *u* element and became a simple *k-* in pronunciation although it was spelled *qu-: quando > quant, quod > que*. An initial *s-* followed by a consonant (and called *s* impure) was difficult for a late Vulgar Latin speaker to pronounce: he prefixed an *i-* or *e-: spiritus > ispirtus*. The Germanic initial *w-*, in loan words into Romance, became first *gu-*, then gradually the *u* element was eliminated (as with *qu-*) and the *u* was no longer written: *waidanjan > guagnier > gagnier*.

Consonants completely final — either last in a word or becoming so after the loss of a final vowel — were in a weak position. The labials *p, b, v* usually became *f* in the final position: *cap (u) > chief, seb (u) > sie̯j, viv (u) > vif*, but rarely they became *-u: cap (u) > chieu, sebu > sieu, riv (u) > riu*. The dentals *d* and *t* were both represented by final *t*, before the year 1000: *nud (u) > nut, dat (u) > det.*[12] Final *c* was frequently dropped during Vulgar Latin: *hoc > o*, but, in general, we may say that final *-c* and *-g* are usually found as *i* at the close of the Low Romance period: *(il)lac > lai* (unless the final vowel was so slow in dropping that a *c* developed as a medial: *pace > pais*), *leg (e) > lei*. The consonants *l, n, r, s* were unchanged in the final position. An *m* often shifted to *n*, but this was not an in-

---

[12] This *t* dropped later, in Old French. See § 29 A.

variable change: *hom* (*o*) > *on* or *om*. We have remarked on page 35 that a consonant coming immediately after another consonant, with which it does not combine intimately, was not apt to alter — just as was the case with an initial. This continued to be true with such a consonant becoming final, but, if voiced, it unvoiced: *salv* (*u*) > *salf, sangu* (*e*) > *sanc, but col* (*a*)*p* (*u*) > *colp, salt* (*u*) > *salt*.

In the medial position (between two vowels) *p, b, v* were weakening a bit in Vulgar Latin; they became β and then *v* in the course of Low Romance: *ripa* > *rive, faba* > *feve, levame* > *levain*. However, before an accented *u* or *o* this β did not shift to *v* but was absorbed into the accented vowel: *tabone* > *taon, pavone* > *paon*. Medial *t* and *d* both became a weak *dh* sound (like English *th* in *this*) although usually spelled *d: nuda* > *nude, amata* > *amede*.[13] Medial *c* and *g* before the vowels *o* and *u* disappeared: *legume* > *leun, securu* > *seur*. Before an *a* they both became a *i̯: pacare* > *pai̯ier, plaga* > *plaie*. A *g* before *e* and *i* had already changed to a *i̯*, in Vulgar Latin; a *c* before *e* and *i* became *is: racemu* > *raisin*. The consonants *l, m, n, r* remained visibly unchanged. A medial *s* was pronounced as a *z* but continued an *s* in spelling.

We are now concerned with consonants in combination. All double consonants became single at the very close of the Low Romance period, shortly before 1000 — too late for the new single consonant to undergo any change whatsoever, and too late to allow a preceding vowel to act as though free: *cattu* > *chat, troppu* > *trop, cappa* > *chape*.[14] We must next consider those consonant groups where an intimate combination was made — where the second element was **not** to be treated as an initial. This is nearly always the case with a consonant plus *i̯* or *yod: ci̯* > *c* (pron. *ts*) or *–z* when final, *gi̯* and *di̯* > *i̯* (in Vulgar Latin), *fi̯* > *iff, li̯* > *–ill–* or *–il* (pronounced a palatal *l*),[15] *ni̯* > *ign* or *–ing* (pron. palatal *n*), *mni̯* or *mmi̯* > *ng* (pron. *nj* as in English " conjure "), *pi̯* > *ch, bi̯* and *vi̯* > *g* (pron. as English *j*), *ti̯* > *is* (with *s* as a *z*), *ri̯* > *ir*,[16] *si̯* > *is: facia* > *face, hodie* > *ui, corri̯gia* > *courreie,* *kofia* > *coiffe, aliu* > *ail, animalia* > *aumaille, companione* > *compaignon* but *companio* > *compaing, commeatu* > *congiet, apiu* > *ache, tibia* > *tige, paria* > *paire, serviente* > *sergent, potione* > *poison, ma* (*n*)*sione* > *maison*. It is occasionally

---

[13] See § 29 A for further change in Old French.

[14] A double *r*, double *l*, or double *n* combination might continue to be written in individual cases.

[15] *–il* was the result when the palatal became final by loss of a vowel: *–ill–* was the spelling when the *l* remained medial; the same distinction held for *–ing* and *–ign–*.

[16] The suffix *ariu* had an irregular treatment: *ier* was the invariable result.

true that the speakers failed to make an intimate combination between a consonant and a *i̯*, in which case the *i̯* > *g* as though it were initial: *al/eam* > *alge, li/ne̯u* > *linge.*

The combinations of a consonant plus a *u̯* (like English *w*) are not frequent except in preterites: *habui, sapui,* etc. The rule here was that the first consonant was lost (except in *lu̯* and *nu̯*) and the *u* remained, combining with the previous vowel: *(h)abuisti* > **auist* > *oüst, potui* > *poi.* Some words (not preterites) show the *u* remaining as a *v,* when after the main accent: *vi̯dua* > *veve.* Examples of *lu̯* and *nu̯* are *annuale* > *anvel, voluit* > **volvt* > *volt* (it is obvious that the *v* must finally drop in this awkward position between two consonants).

The following are combinations with *l: -cl-* and *-gl-* > *-ill-* or *-il* (the palatal *l*), *-pl-* and *-bl-* > *-bl-, -ml-* > *-mbl-:* *auri̯c(u)la* > *oreille, pari̯c(u)lu* > *pareil, reg(u)la* > *reille, ne̯b(u)la* > *nieble, pop(u)lu* > *pueble, cum(u)lu* > *comble.* The *r* combinations are: *-pr-, -br-, -vr-* > **-βr-* > *-vr-; -tr-* and *-dr-* > *-dr-* (with *d* like *th* in *this*); *-cr-* and *-gr-* > *-ir-; -nr-* > *-ndr-; -mr-* > *-mbr; -lr-* > *-ldr-; -sr-* > *-str.* Examples are: *capra* > *chievre, labra* > *levre, viv(e)re* > *vivre, patre* > *pedre, quadratu* > *quadret, lacrima* > *lairme, ni̯gru* > *neir, ci̯n(e)re* > *cendre, cam(e)ra* > *chambre, fal'rat* (< *fallere abet*) > *faldrat, mis'runt* > *mistrent.*

The next heading is that of miscellaneous consonant combinations. When a group of three consonants results from sundry vowel omissions it is usual for the center consonant to go: *dorm(i)t* > *dort.* When two consonants of different articulation (labial and dental, for example) come together as a result of vowel dropping, the first consonant is apt to be affected by the second: *sem(i)ta* > *sente.* The group *-ct-* (and *-gd-*), very common, already changed in Vulgar Latin times to *-it-* (and *-id-*): *lactuca* > *laitu(i)e.* Note that the ending *–aticu,* which is common, develops constantly into *–age: coraticu* > *corage.* Often the ending *–alis,* which should change according to rule into *-els,* remains *–als,* through **semilearned** influence: *ripale* > *rival* and not **rivel;* even so *–abilis* usually gives *–ables* and not the *–ebles* which we should expect: *cantabilis* > *chantables* and not **chantebles.* It is difficult to observe a rule for the treatment of Latin *x.* Three results are discernible, *s, ss* or *is: exagium* > *essai, extra* > *estre, *ex'ere* > **ieistre* > *istre.* It would be well for the student to expect any one of the three.

17. THE SPORADIC PHENOMENA

There are certain phenomena of an uncertain nature which occasionally disturbed the normal " drift " that we have outlined. One of these is **aphæresis**, in which an initial sound of a word became confused with a preceding article and was removed from the word permanently: *la raigne* for *l'araigne* (cf. English *orange < norange* and *adder < nadder*). There was a phenomenon opposite to aphæresis which we commonly call **prosthesis**: *lierre < l'ierre*. In **metathesis** the relative order of sounds — adjacent or nonadjacent — became confused: *torbler < trobler* (cf. English *Caliban < canibal*). In **assimilation** a sound, usually a liquid or nasal, was attracted to another similar sound in a nearby position: *nofferai < non-ferai*. **Dissimilation** was the opposite phenomenon to this: *multrir < murtrir*. Sometimes a whole syllable, or several, could be omitted by dissimilation: *ar (te ma)tematica > artimaire* in Old French). This we call **haplology**. The reasons for such mistakes as these — because they were originally only errors in speech — are not difficult to divine. Illiterate people are always liable to error, since they cannot stabilize their speech through reading, and the average Low Romance or Old French speaker was illiterate.

18. ADAPTATION OF THE PASSAGE FROM PETRONIUS

We now continue the adaption of the passage from Petronius, introduced in the preceding chapter. Here we turn it into Old French of the year 1000 — after the Romance drift has had its way.

Oiens ruit estrange desoz la mestre chambre com ruit d'une beste qui istre vuelt. Siveins donc lo son si trovons Eumolpe qui siet avant un grant perchemin e escrit vers. Miret sons que li leüst chantique faire, morte vedant, si lo traieins en avant plourant e li mandons vienget a raison. Mais lui bien troblez entrat en grant ire si dist: Laissiez mei mes diz traire a fin; fin de dit est dure. Jo met main a lui plein de rage e mant a Gidone de venir e traire lo trovedour a terre.

There are some important syntactical changes here from the Vulgar Latin. Note that the article *lo* is more common than Vulgar Latin *illo;* note also the frequency of *si* (from German *so* and *thanne* constructions). The *sons* is from *sumus*. *Mirati* has become *miret* but this participle can no longer stand without a copula. The *morte vedant* is an absolute construction of a type very common in Old French, meaning " with Death looking on."

19. EXERCISES

For those who wish to learn the rules of the Romance " drift " given in § 16 we add some words for practice.

I. Give the intermediate stages by which

sémita	>	*sente*	path
reputáre	>	*reter*	accuse
plácitu	>	*plait*	argument
insúbulum	>	*ensuble*	weaver's beam
mediánu	>	*moiien*	middle
mędiu	>	*mi*	middle
cįnere	>	*cendre*	ash
artemįsia	>	*armoise*	wormwood
insįmul	>	*ensemble*	together
clausióne	>	*cloison*	enclosure
calceáre	>	*chaucier*	shod
prętiu	>	*pris*	worth
crįppia	>	*creche*	crib
apiáriu	>	*achier*	parsley
ápe	>	*ef*	bee
serviénte	>	*sergent*	serving man
cambiáre	>	*changier*	change
sabúcu	>	*seu*	elderberry tree

II. Trace into Old French, remembering that you may not recognize the result as a *modern* French form: *fídus, flámmula, mánica, bárba, cervĭce, náusea, càpitális, captĭvu, vetáre, pàstináca, árca, ǔnquam, wardáre* (Frankish *wardôn), *gállu, pĕde, cáru, cárru, córpus, bráca, factĭciu, féria, júliu, mŏdiu, pérsica, dòrmitóriu, caldária, còmputáre, cápsa, prŏpe, fáme, addéntes.*

Examples: *gémmula* > V. L. **įemmla* > O. Fr. *gemble; cùmuláre* > V. L. **comlare* > O. F. *combler; còmmeátum* > V. L. **commįatu* > O. F. *congiet; aprįlem* > O. F. *avril; camįnus* > O. F. *chemins.*

REFERENCES

MULLER, H. F., " A Chronology of Vulgar Latin," Beiheft no. 78 of the *ZfrPh* (1929).

VENDRYES, J., in *Rev. Ling. Rom.,* I (on Celtic influences).

BRÜCH, J., *Ibid.*, II, 30–45 (on Germanic influence).

SJÖGREN, A., in *Romania*, LIV, 381–412 (on Norse element).

FOERSTER, W., and KOSCHWITZ, E., *Altfranzösisches Übungsbuch*, (6th ed., Leipzig: Reisland, 1921).

VOSSLER, K., *Frankreichs Kultur in Spiegel seiner Sprachentwicklung* (3rd ed., Heidelberg: Winter, 1927).

And the numerous works on Old French phonology published by Schwan-Behrens, Meyer-Lübke, Bourciez, and others.

IV

OLD FRENCH

(1000–1300)

20. CIVILIZATION

During the eleventh century medieval civilization expanded its horizon. Hitherto the direction of man's thought had been backward towards the glory of Rome and towards the asceticism of the Church; but after the year 1000, although these things were not forgotten, there was a branching forth of activity towards new things. Led by the spirit of the Normans who had settled in Normandy, there were pious crusades, and expeditions not so pious, into Spain, Sicily, Great Britain, Byzantium, and the Holy Land. More buildings began to be built in stone, and the old Roman basilica type of architecture was supplanted by the Romanesque of southern France. Even the art of painting or illumination of MSS. became more graceful and the use of gold leaf more frequent. We have about forty beautifully tooled book bindings from the twelfth century. Such a thing would have been unheard of in the tenth century. Philosophic speculation became active and more original during the course of the eleventh century, when the problems of scholasticism took form under Anselm, Roscellin, and Abelard. The educated or clerical class increased its numbers in unparalleled fashion. Not all these clerics intended to be monks or priests, as was often the case in the earlier Middle Ages. Instead many of them became teachers of profane literature, minstrels, civil lawyers, professional copyists, booksellers, and even accountants.[1] Those who *did* take priest's orders often served as schoolmasters to the laity, both men and women. Thus learning came out from the shelter of the cloister, to a certain extent, and even the ignorant became literarily minded.

21. LITERATURE

In the Low Romance period the populace sang their ballads and their dance songs, but these were condemned by the clergy. If

---

[1] This has survived in modern English (through the Anglo-Norman) when we speak of a "shop clerk" or "hotel clerk."

other amusements were desired one could listen to an occasional saint's life; and, on feast occasions certain scenes from the Bible or saints' legends might be dramatized. Most of these were in Latin with only an occasional condescension towards the laymen by a rendering in the vernacular. It is safe to conjecture that the rank and file of the populace in France depended for entertainment solely upon jugglers, dancers, acrobats, and animal tamers. Literature looked backward — to Rome and to the Church.

But after 1000 there was a change. The *chansons de geste*, or epics, arose along the pilgrim routes. The owner of a castle, as well as the laborer in the market place, thrilled to the heroic and impossible adventures of a Roland or of a William Shortnose. In Normandy and in Anglo-Norman England there was beginning a scientific interest among the lay folk. Lapidaries, calendars, and chronicles were adapted for their delectation. Then by the middle of the twelfth century the romance, an up-to-date imitation of the Latin epic, got a firm hold upon the laymen — and most probably upon the laywomen, who delighted in love and tales of the marvelous. The humble stories of the peasants were dignified with a poetic form and called *fabliaux*. A whole series of animal characters made up the branches of the *Roman de Renart*. Minstrels decided to follow in the footsteps of their brother poets in southern France and composed lyric poetry of a more elevated nature than what was to be found in crude peasant ballads. There was even some clever satire as in the *Roman de Renart* and in *Aucassin et Nicolette* (*c.* 1200). This great revival of activity in all lines is often called the twelfth-century Renaissance, because originality reached its peak during that century; but the beginnings must be placed not far from the year 1000.

22. THE STANDARD OLD FRENCH LANGUAGE

When a people's speech acquires a literature there begins standardization. This fact we stressed in our earlier chapters. The " drift " undergoes a considerable check, although some change must continue, until illiteracy among the people reaches a negligible quantity — which was by no means the case in the twelfth-century Renaissance, when still only a few could read. A need was felt for a standard dialect, as a common medium for this new literature. In the first half of the twelfth century the dialects used in Paris and in Normandy were not too dissimilar, and they formed the basis for a somewhat standard tongue. As the twelfth century progressed some Picardisms were admitted, and when we reach the thirteenth century we even find a standard Picard dialect in use beside the earlier literary dialect. But the Picard was not tolerated long and by the close of the thirteenth century the standard purified dialect was in control in literature.[2]

23 A. THE DIALECT *KOINÉS*

Beside this recognized literary Old French there existed scores of patois throughout the extent of northern France; but very few of these are preserved in literature. In certain important regions a *koiné* or generalized dialect was recognized and certain writers who did not know, or who scorned, the literary French (based upon the *koinés* of Normandy and Paris) used these dialect *koinés*. But, when we say Norman, Anglo-Norman Picard, Francian, Walloon, Lotharingian, or Champenois literature, we do not mean that all Picards, or all Champenois, actually spoke the same dialect; we mean that their individual patois were pooled into one variety commonly understood in that region and that, in the cases in point, this regional speech was used rather than the artificial literary standard. Pure Norman and pure Francian did not continue to be identical with standard Old French, although the latter was originally based upon them and continued to receive some influence.

On the accompanying map we have indicated where these regional *koinés* prevailed. As this map is adapted from the *Atlas linguistique de la France* of Gilliéron and Edmont, the small figures, scattered throughout, indicate individual dialects. Note how numerous these individual dialects are as compared with the main regional *koinés*. The dotted line divides the French speakers (to the north) from the Provençal speakers (to the south). It is more than likely that the course of this dotted line was quite different in the twelfth century from what it is now.

23 B. ANGLO-NORMAN [3]

To English-speaking students one of these dialect *koinés* — the Anglo-Norman — has special significance. Even in the days of

---

[2] *Cf.* Gertrud Wacker's *Dialekt und Schriftsprache im altfranzösischen*, Berlin diss., 1916.

[3] A splendid reference is the little *Anglo-Norman Language and Literature* (London, 1923) of Johan Vising. See also Part V of M. K. Pope's *From Latin to Modern French* (Manchester, 1934).

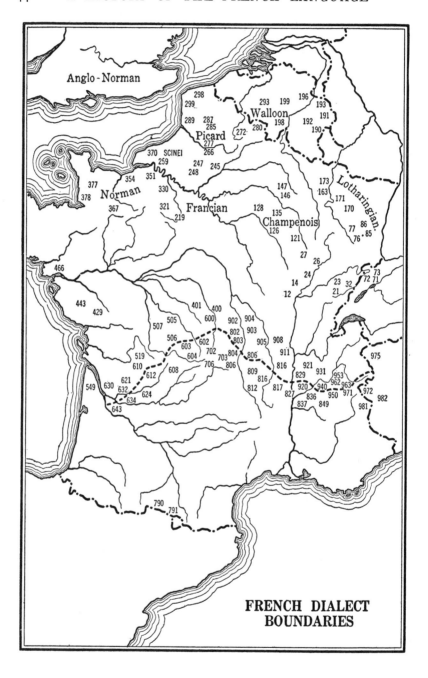

FRENCH DIALECT
BOUNDARIES

Edward the Confessor (reigned 1042–1066) knowledge of the Nor-man-French speech was becoming more and more common in England, as Edward was very pro-Norman. With the conquest of the land by William the Conqueror, in 1066, the Norman dialect was placed on a superior footing. It must be remembered that many of the invaders married English women and that the children of these men doubtless had English nurses. It is to be assumed, therefore, that the Anglo-Normans of the second generation were bilingual.[4] With bilingual speakers (who are not careful gramma-rians) there is apt to be a mutual influence upon each other of the two languages. A peculiar variety of Norman modified by the Germanic habits of English speech took definite shape in the course of the twelfth century. It came to be despised in the thirteenth century when families of rank sought native French teachers; and in the fourteenth we know how disparagingly Chaucer refers to the French dialect of " Stratford-atte-Bowe." In 1362 Edward III abolished the use of French in parliamentary proceedings; this was the deathblow to Anglo-Norman, save for loanwords in English.

Of the influence of Norman French on English we can say that before 1250 not more than five hundred French words can be found in English written texts, but in the spoken English of the period the number must have been far greater.

24. METHODS OF OBSERVATION

Because we are dependent upon the written word for our knowl-edge of Old French we are mostly concerned with the so-called standard speech. We cannot fully trust the *koiné* literature as evidence of dialect — because there too we find artificiality. About the only accurate dialect criteria that we possess for this early period are legal papers that can be dated and located with cer-tainty. Behrens has collected an excellent group of these as a third division to the Schwan-Behrens *Grammatik der altfranzösischen Sprache*. But our chief interest, none the less, will lie with the stand-ard language of the period. In the preceding chapter we recorded the " drift " as it affected the Francian dialect, which was the chief element in the formation of literary Old French.

In observing the development of literary French, from this point

---

[4] In the case of the king, and of other families who retained their chief residence in Normandy proper, this was not necessarily the case till after the loss of Normandy by the English crown in 1204.

on, we shall be concerned with certain lexicographical details: the systems of spelling used, the source of new words borrowed into the language (foreign, learned, dialect, manufactured, jargon words), use of punctuation and accents, existing dictionaries and grammars. We shall not neglect either the outstanding alterations of syntax, morphology, and semantics. Versification must receive some attention. These, with phonology, are the main items in the study of linguistics.

25. OLD FRENCH VOCABULARY

The Latin spoken by the educated class, the clergy, furnished most of the *new* words adopted into standard French during this period. W. M. McLeod, under the direction of one of the authors, examined 1271 words which were borrowed into Old French directly from Latin in the eleventh and twelfth centuries. He found the distribution of these words, according to meaning, as follows: ecclesiastical terms — 351, legal — 153, terms of government — 16, commerce — 11, military — 10, social — 5, amusement — 2, heraldry — 1, naval — 1, general science — 324, literature and language — 104, philosophy — 68, music — 50, magic — 2, the body — 13, family — 11, common household terms — 8, agriculture — 7, dress — 8, sustenance — 5, games — 4, unproductive callings — 2, town — 1, determinant qualities — 98, indeterminant qualities — 41, non-classifiable — 20. These learned words (not to be confused with the semilearned of the previous chapter) show how the influence of the clergy was felt by the average layman. Greek was an unknown language despite the crusades. An occasional word was brought back from Constantinople, and some medical terms such as *catimini* were met with; but these could not have affected many people. After Latin, the second greatest influence during this period was from Provençal — the language spoken in France south of the dotted line on the map of dialect *koinés*. Many of the expressions were borrowed from the southern troubadours who sang of love and liaisons: *amor, amoros, jalos* (jealous), *espos* (husband). There were others of a general abstract nature: *abelir* (to please), *anbelir* (to beautify), *desabelir* (to displease), *m'est bel* (it pleases me), *m'est bon, aferir* (to concern), *goloser* (to covet), *atiser* (to inflame), *blandir* (to flatter), *donoier* (to flirt), *esbatre* (to amuse oneself), *muser* (to gape idly), *abet* (ruse), *barat* (cheat), *barate* (confusion), *desbareter* (to destroy), *guile, tafur* (rascal), *trufe* (deceit), *boban* (arrogance) *ba-*

lais (spinel ruby), *dangier* (resistance), *solaz* (comfort), *gai, jolif* (gay), *poli, sordeis* (worst), *noalz* (worthless), *malade*. Others were concrete: *cembel* (ambush), *guimple, rossignol* (nightingale), *meschin*, (youth), *tose* (girl), *trescier* (to dance), *lai* (song), *ribaut* (ruffian), *truant* (beggar); and still others are difficult to classify: *ades* (constantly), *viste* (quickly), *igal* (equal).[5] Note how the words borrowed from Provence, if Braun's list is representative, are upperclass words, proper for the knight and lady rather than for the bourgeois and peasant.

A few Arabic words drifted into French at this time: some through Italian, from the Norman kingdom in Sicily and southern Italy, others through Provençal, from Spain and from the Arabic settlers in southern France. Perhaps some words of this sort were introduced directly by French travelers from Spain and the Holy Land. There are forms such as *tabor, meschin*, and the fantastic *algalife* and *amuaffle*.

We have already stated that numerous dialect forms were used in standard Old French: *biaus, gatax*, and the like, but this was a tendency too general to be estimated. It is also extremely difficult to take account of the Germanic words that came in during the Old French period. The Anglo-Normans in England used many Middle English words and scores of these doubtless passed into use on the mainland: *biet, gotelef, loc*. From Germany proper the borrowing was much less pronounced. The political and literary relations with Germany were no longer active, except when they ran the other way; viz., the Germans adapted many French poems into their own language. The French were afraid of Frederick Barbarossa and, except for the Count of Champagne and other border counts, intimacy was avoided. However, *seneschal, mareschal, eschanson* are words of German origin, admitted into French during the twelfth century, but possibly from a Latinized German form. From the continental Bretons an occasional word came into French use: *carole, ha*, " and," in *Guildeluec ha Guilliadun* of Marie's *Eliduc* (v. 22); but such Breton borrowings were more apt to be proper names found in the literary romances of the twelfth century. There was virtually no borrowing from Italian and Spanish vernaculars.

[5] We are citing the lists given by Georg Braun in his "Der Einfluss des südfranzösischen Minnesangs und Ritterwesens auf die nordfranzösische Sprache bis zum 13[t]. Jahrhundert," *Romanische Forschungen*, March, 1929, pp. 1–160.

26. MORPHOLOGY

The unique characteristic of Old French morphology is the two-case system retained from Vulgar Latin. Although evidence shows that writers were sometimes careless in the use of the nominative and objective cases, the distinction was never completely disregarded. There were three declensions:

	1st *Singular*	*2nd* *Singular*	*3rd* *Singular*
Nom.	la fille	li murs	li lerre, la suer
Obj.	la fille	le mur	le larron, la serour
	Plural	*Plural*	*Plural*
Nom.	les filles	li mur	li larron, les serours
Obj.	les filles	les murs	les larrons, les serours

The third declension had two types: a masculine and a feminine. The adjectives used the endings of the first declension for the feminine form, and those of the second for the masculine: *bons, bone, etc.* There was one type of adjective, derived from the Latin third declension, which did not add an *e* in the feminine: Masc. *granz, grant, grant, granz,* Fem. *grant, grant, granz, granz.*[6] Compare such forms with the paradigm given above and observe the difference and similarity. If the stem of a noun or adjective ends normally in *t*, the ending −*s*, when added, contracts with the *t* to form a *z* (still pronounced *ts*); e.g., *grant* + *s* > *granz*. When the stem ends in *c, f, b,* or *p,* the added −*s* causes the end consonant to be dropped; *gab* + *s* > *gas, chief* + *s* > *chies, sac* + *s* > *sas, colp* + *s* > *cols* > *cous*. From this last example observe that in the combination *ls* the *l* vocalizes to a *u*, during the course of the twelfth century.

As an example of the Old French verb paradigm we are giving the first conjugation in full, on the opposite page. There were three normal conjugations, as in modern French, the −*er* and −*ier* verbs, the −*ir* verbs, and the −*re* verbs. There were some additional verbs in −*oir* not to be counted as a separate conjugation.

27. SYNTAX

Three qualities of Old French syntax are always in evidence: asyndetism, determinism, and inconsistent use of the tenses. In

---

[6] This explains modern French *grand'chose, grand'mère*. The apostrophe indicates that the modern speaker does not understand the lack of the *e*.

plainer language, the first means that clauses are related to each other very carelessly, most often with a *que* (to be translated " that, so that, for, because, since," etc.) or with an *ains* best translated as " rather." The use of *si* (< Germanic *so* and *thanne* constructions) was also worked overtime. By determinism we mean the language is plainly demonstrative: *es vous le roi qui vient!*, where modern French would prefer *Le roi vient.* Thirdly, there was no question of sequence of tenses.

The remaining forms were made periphrastically with the past participle *chantez* (*chanté; chantee*) or with the present participle *chantanz* with the aid of auxiliaries: *avoir, estre,* or *aler.*

Other striking characteristics are the preferred use of infinitives as nouns: *avoirs* (money), *mangiers* (dinner), and certain word orders. Whereas in modern French the order *subject + predicate + complement — Le roi voit le chevalier —* is almost obligatory, Old French had two other word orders to be employed in prescribed cases: *subject + complement + predicate* (in subordinate clauses): *qui le chevalier voit,* and *predicate + subject + complement* (to be used after an adverb): *A certes voit li rois le chevalier.*

Many of the modern French idioms are the survival of normal Old French expressions: *ne* (*mais*) . . . *que,* " no more . . . than," now rendered by " only "; *I a du pain* (*assez*) " there is a sufficiency of bread " which, with the adverb of quantity omitted, is now called the partitive construction; *Et lui d'aler* (*ne fina*) " And he did not cease going," which is now called the historical infinitive.

28. VERSIFICATION

All early literature is apt to be in verse. Poetry is more easily memorized than prose and at the beginnings of a people's literature few individuals can read; they depend upon recitation from memory by minstrels. The eight-syllable line was perhaps the first meter in Old French literature and was derived from the Latin hexameter. This verse scheme continued to be used in the saints' lives, romances, and tales. A variation was the ten-syllable line, with an internal pause or cæsura after the fourth syllable. This became the favorite in the *chansons de geste.* The line of twelve syllables, or alexandrine, was introduced early in the Old French period, but it found little favor, till after 1200, when the reading public was larger. Apparently the twelve-syllable line, with a cæsura in the middle, was not adapted to recitation. The earliest Old French literature was in

First Conjugation
Chanter

Indicative		*Subjunctive*	

Present

je chant	nos chantons	je chant	nos chantions
tu chantes	vos chantez	tu chanz	vos chantiez
il chante	il chantent	il chant	il chantent

Imperfect

1.
je chantoe	nos chantions	je chantasse	nos chantissions
tu chantoes	vos chantiez	tu chantasses	vos chantissiez
il chantot	il chantoent	il chantast	il chantassent

2.
je chantoie	nos chantions
tu chantoies	vos chantiez
il chantoit	il chantoient

Future

je chanterai	nos chanterons
tu chanteras	vos chanteroiz
il chantera	il chanteront

Conditional

chanteroie	chanterions
chanteroies	chanteriez
chanteroit	chanteroient

Preterite

chantai	chantames
chantas	chantastes
chanta	chanterent

rhymed stanzas; very quickly *laisses* (stanzas of varying length) became the rule for the epics, where assonance replaced rhyme. The romances and tales preferred the rhymed couplet. After 1200 assonance gave way to rhymed *laisses* in the epics.

29 A. PROGRESS OF THE "DRIFT" DURING THE OLD FRENCH PERIOD

We have remarked that the rise of Old French literature slowed down further change in the sounds of French. This is true, but a few changes managed to slip through. After 1050 medial and final *d* and *t* dropped away: *vedant > veant, piet > pié*. In the third person endings of verb forms this *t* was sometimes retained to avoid confusion: *chiet*. Also free accented *ou* (< *ǫ*) > *eu: doulour > douleur*. During the course of the twelfth century *ei* (< *ę*) > *oi*, except in England and in Normandy: *mei > moi; l* before a consonant vocalized to a *u: salt > saut; iu > ui: riu > rui, siu > sui*. In etymologizing a word from the Latin into Old French, remember the three sets of changes: those of Vulgar Latin, those of Low Romance, and those taking place in the Old French period itself. The second group is by far the largest.

29 B. JUDÆO-FRENCH

The Jews in medieval France lived in closely associated communities, often from choice rather than from persecution. They had their own schools and universities. Although they spoke French habitually, the learned influence on the language was Hebrew rather than Latin, and so there came into their speech many specialized meanings and phonetic developments which were slightly different from those of their Christian neighbors. Our knowledge of this Judæo-French is derived mostly from glosses or notes made in French (with Hebrew letters) on the margin, or between the lines, of Hebrew manuscripts. Arsène Darmesteter and the late D. S. Blondheim were among the leading scholars who studied these glosses.[7]

30. TRANSLATION

In closing this chapter we render our passage from Petronius into the Old French of the year 1200. Aside from the few phono-

---

[7] For a convenient list of Judæo-French words consult Raphael Levy's *Recherches lexicographiques sur d'anciens textes français d'origine juive* (Baltimore, 1932).

logical and morphological changes, there is a variation in style and choice of vocabulary under the growing literary influence:

Ja somes pensif por oir un bruit merveilleus qui vient de desoz la mestre chambre de la nef com cel d'une beste qui istre vuelt. Lors querons tant que veomes Eumolpe qui seoit delez un grant parchemin e qui en rimoier s'entent. A merveille le tenons que li leüst chançon faire, mort veant, si'l traions en avant, qui crie e brait, e si li mandons de venir a sen. Mais lui ert si courreciez qu'il entra en grant ire si dist: Laissiez moi mes diz traire a fin; mar quiert hom vers a parachever. Je met force a l'enragié e mant a Gione de venir e metre a terre le trouveür.

REFERENCES

BEAULIEUX, CHARLES, *Histoire de l'orthographe française* (2 vols.; Paris: Champion, 1927).

FOULET, LUCIEN, *Petite syntaxe de l'ancien français* (3rd ed.; Paris: Champion, 1930).

GODEFROY, FRÉDÉRIC (and BONNARD, J., and SALMON, A.), *Lexique de l'ancien français* (1 vol.; Paris: Welter, 1901).

BLOCH, O., and VON WARTBURG, W., *Dictionnaire étymologique de la langue française* (Paris: Les Presses Universitaires de France, 1932).

FOUCHÉ, P., *Le verbe français* (Paris: Belles Lettres, 1931).

TOBLER, A., *Vom französischen Versbau* (5th ed.; Leipzig: Hirzel, 1910).

LEVY, RAPHAEL, *Répertoire des lexiques du vieux français* (New York: Mod. Lang. Assoc., 1937).

V

THE MIDDLE FRENCH PERIOD
(1300–1515)

31. CIVILIZATION

Generally speaking, these two hundred years saw the decline of medieval institutions. In 1291 the Saracens recaptured the town of Akka, or Saint-Jean-d'Acre, and the crusaders withdrew for good from the Holy Land. The authority of the papacy was badly shaken by the withdrawal of the popes to Avignon (1309–1377) and by the Great Schism of 1378–1417, during which, at one time, there were as many as three popes! Add to this the fact that the wealth and laxity of the clergy became so flagrant that bandits and perjurors could find no better field of activity than under the Church's banners, and it is understandable why thousands of individuals lost their faith. The Church, the greatest force for peace and order during the earlier centuries, no longer held supreme sway. Surely this explains the decay of medieval civilization. The system of thinking was altering also. The schoolmen of the twelfth and thirteenth centuries were realists — that is, they believed in the *real* prior existence of the world's plan and of its virtues in the mind of God, before Creation — and consequently they trusted implicitly in the authority of God and of those inspired by God in the knowledge and conduct of affairs. Beginning with an Englishman, William of Occam (1270–1347), this realism was replaced by a nominalism which denied the premises of prior existence.[1] This lead to outright materialism and to a distrust in authority. Thus the schools themselves prepared the minds of men for the scepticism of the coming humanists. So pronounced was the increasing lack of faith, in the fifteenth century, that those hundred years are often characterized as the century of Death. The mind of the fifteenth-century man was haunted by the fear of dying, unrelieved by faith in the Great Unknown. This was soon counterbalanced by the paganism of the

[1] First suggested by Roscellinus, in the late eleventh century, who was obliged to recant.

following Renaissance which taught men to concentrate upon life while they had it.

Other unfavorable factors during this Middle French period were the devastating Hundred Years' War with England (1337–1453) and the consequent crowding of the rural population into cities. Year after year the English armies burned and pillaged in northern and southwestern France while the French withdrew to the protection of strong walls and waited for their foes to retire. Everywhere except in the capital cities at the courts of the mighty lords conditions became unfavorable for the production of literature and for the cultivation of the French language. The poet became a mere hired retainer.

Having painted this very dark picture in general, we must call attention to one patch of light. The reign of Charles V (1364–1380) encouraged letters and a considerable intercourse with Italy. The pope was at Avignon during most of the fourteenth century and the papal *Curia* included many Italians. Charles V married his son, Louis of Touraine (later of Orléans), to Valentine, daughter of the Visconti at Milan. Such prominent Frenchmen as Gontier Col, Bersuire, Oresme, and Gerson spent time at Avignon; others — Philippe de Mezières, Jacques le Grand, and Jean de Montreuil — spent months in Italy. The king and his brother, the Duke of Berry, had magnificent libraries. This brief Italian renaissance could not bear fruit because of the disastrous conditions which followed immediately during the reign of Charles VI (1380–1422), the mad king.

32. THE RISE OF THE LAWYER

Saint Louis, King Louis IX (1226–1270), thoroughly reformed legal practices in France. These reforms are usually dated c 1260 but it is quite probable that they were slightly earlier. Chief among these was permission for testimony to be presented in writing, allowing the principal parties to be absent while represented by professional lawyers. Appeals to the central courts at Paris were encouraged. Experts in civil law began to multiply at an enormous rate. Towards the close of the thirteenth century Philip the Fair gave up his royal palace, on the Cité, to the royal *Curia* — the courts of justice. Although this original palace has disappeared, except for portions of the ground floor and except for the marvelous Ste Chapelle, the site is occupied by the present Palais de Justice.

The lawyers had clerks who flocked to Paris in extraordinary numbers. The original king's *Curia* divided into various courts during the course of the thirteenth century — into *Parlement*, the *Grand Conseil*, and the *Chambre des Comptes*. Beneath these was the local provost's court of the city of Paris, which was a strictly local affair. It was called the *Châtelet* because it had its head-quarters in an old city gate of that name.[2] The clerks of the *Châtelet* organized a society called a *bazoche*. This idea spread until there was a *bazoche* for the *Chambre des Comptes* and a *bazoche* for the clerks of *Parlement*. Then the various local courts throughout France organized *bazoches* also for their unmarried clerks. The *bazoche* of *Parlement*, though it was not the oldest, insisted upon taking first place among these societies. The importance of the *bazoches* in the development of the French drama does not concern us here. But it is these same lawyers' clerks who deformed the spelling of the French language during the Middle French period.

33. SPELLING

The *conseillers* (solicitors), *procureurs* (barristers), notaries, and their clerks, were required to know some Latin, except in the lower courts. Although the pleas and indictments were in French, the decrees and legal codes were couched in a hybrid barbarous Latin. This bilingualism continued until the decree made by King Francis I at Villers-Cotterets in 1539, abolishing Latin from the courts. Since the clerks seldom had much learning, it was not long before they mixed their Latin and their French in spelling, vocabulary, and syntax. Noting the resemblance between Latin *dictum* and French *dit*, they wrote *dict* in French; similarly, because of *lego*, French *lais* began to be written *legs; doit* became *doigt* under influence from *digitus*, and *vint* was written *vingt*, after *viginti*. These etymological spellings soon spread beyond the range of law documents. They were adopted by the poets and other men of letters during the fourteenth century and continued thereafter for centuries to come. We quote a few passages from François Villon to illustrate his use of these queer spellings:

> Et se j'ay *prins* en ma faveur
> Ces *doulx* regars et beaux semblans (*Lais*, 25–26),

[2] Cf. the Newgate of London.

S'il ne le *scet,* voise l'aprendre (*Testament,* 38),
Ma vielle ay mys *soubz* le banc (*ibid.,* 717),
Si en *escrips* au collateur (*ibid.,* 1330).

We leave to the student the task of determining what Latin word influenced those forms which we have italicized. In addition to etymological spellings, *un* came to be written *ung* and *y* was preferred for *i* (see examples above). The handwriting of the Middle French period had become so conventionalized and difficult to read that it is likely these two spellings were introduced for the sake of clarity. A *y* is more easily read than an *i;* two *i*'s and the *n* and *u* were often confused: the *g* labeled *un* for the rapid gaze of the reader.

34. VOCABULARY

The present writer has had his students make classified counts of the new words admitted to the language during this period. Since the total figures arrived at in such a count are certain to be unreliable we prefer to give only proportionate results. Latin continued to be the commonest source — at least 50 per cent of the new words were adopted from that language: *demolir, denigrer, funeste,* and *alchimie* (from Medieval Latin). A further 10 to 20 per cent of the newly adopted words were existing words made over to resemble more exactly the Latin: *delecter* (< *delectare*) to replace *delitier.* This Latinizing was doubtless emphasized by the patronage of learning during the reign of Charles V. The translator of the Lotharingian Psalter is our authority that " convient que per corruption et per diseite des mos francois que en dit lou romans selonc lou latin sicom *iniquitas* iniquiteit, *redemptio* redemption, etc." [3]

Occasionally a change was made for no discernible reason: *aveline* replacing *avelaine.* Why ? The Latin is *abellana.* From 5 to 12 per cent of the total of new words were adopted from dialect *koinés* (in which we include Provençal): *carogne* (from the Norman), *brume* (from Provençal). These elements total approximately three-fourths of the new vocabulary. The remaining 20 or 30 per cent were adopted from Italian, Flemish, German, Spanish, Arabic, and Greek in descending order of importance. In general we may comment that the Latin borrowings were no longer restricted to the

---

[3] "It is fitting that one say Romance words like the Latin, as *iniquitas, iniquiteit,* . . . because of the corruption and lack of French words."

learned professions, as was apt to be the case in the preceding period. *Clergie* — due to the increase in universities ? — had spread to the other classes in limited degree, if we except the peasants. The remaking of existing words may be attributed to the same conditions that inspired Latinized spelling. The Flemish, German, and Italian words were brought in by mercenary troops during the Hundred Years' War.

35. PRONUNCIATION

The vulgar alterations which we call " drift " continued to a small degree; but the writing public was now too conscious of a standardized language to tolerate this generally. Gradually final consonants were silenced when followed immediately by a word beginning with a consonant: for*t* bien, le*s* dames. Such consonants continued to be pronounced, however, before a following vowel: *les amis*, or before a pause. The vowel *e* was shifted to an *a* before *r*: *merchant > marchant, per > par.* When *ie* followed a palatal the *i* element became lost: *chief > chef.* The sound written *z* in Old French (that is *ts*) was now completely confused with *s*, and *z* had the value of *s* in spelling. The combination *oi* was pronounced in at least three different ways: *oi* (as in English *boy*), [wɛ] (like modern French *ouais!*), [ɛ] (as in modern French *ai*), and perhaps sometimes [wa] (the modern French pronunciation of *oi*). In Old French of the twelfth century *oi* as in English *boy* was the rule. So far as we know the Middle French speaker was governed by circumstance and by individual cases in his choice between these variant pronunciations of *oi*. In such a word as *convent* the *on* had become *ou: couvent.* No one pronounced the extra letters introduced by etymological spellings: *p* in *escripvre*, etc.

36. SYNTAX

This is a problem that has yet to be solved. M. Lucien Foulet renounced his intention of writing a *Petite syntaxe du moyen français* to conform with his study of Old French usage. This is because the Middle French syntax offers so many irregularities. We quote from the writer of the last years of the fourteenth century who translated the Psalms of David (the Lotharingian Psalter):

Nul ne tient en son parleir ne rigle certenne, mesure ne raison, et laingue romance est si corrompue, qu'a poinne li uns entent l'aultre. . . .

Louis B. Stabler has adapted for use in French the Spanish syntax check list of Professor Hayward Keniston of Chicago. With the aid of this valuable instrument a group of University of North Carolina students, including Dr. Stabler, have made some study of the syntax of the fourteenth and fifteenth centuries. From the work completed so far it becomes evident that the chaos is not quite as great as we had previously thought. While exceptions to the tendencies of Old French syntax are growing, it is in the multiplying of dependent clauses, often poorly connected, that the peculiarity of the period lies. We quote from the *Quadrilogue Invectif* (c. 1422) of Alain Chartier as an example to the point.

Comme les haultes dignitez des seigneuries soient establies soubz la divine et infinie puissance qui les eslieve en florissant, en prosperité et en glorieuse renommee, il est a croire et tenir fermement que, ainsi que leurs commencemens et leurs accroissances sont maintenues et adrecees par la divine providence, ainsi est leur fin et leur detriment par sentence donnee ou hault conseil de la souveraine sapience qui les aucuns verse du hault trosne de imperial seigneurie en la basse fosse de servitute et de magnificence en ruine et fait des vainqueurs vaincus et ceuls obeïr par crainte qui commander souloient par autorité.

Such fondness for antitheses and for hesitating structure may well be due to the abuse of logic in the universities; we have mentioned how the instruction of the schools was becoming more and more popular.

37 A. MORPHOLOGY

The case system was completely abandoned during the period 1375 to 1420. The objective case alone was preserved for nearly all common nouns. In the case of personal names the nominative case often survived: *Charles* (not *Charle*). We find double survival in *on* (nom.) and *homme* (obj.) of modern French; also in *gars, garçon, copain, compagnon, sire, seigneur*. Examples of the old nominative surviving in common nouns are to be found in *fils, sœur, chantre, peintre, pastre, prestre*, and *traistre*, in the place of *fil, sereur, chanteeur, peinteur, pasteur, provaire, traiteur*. The *chanteur* and *pasteur* which survive today are later formations of a different origin. Adjectives which did not take a feminine *e* in Old French began to do so in the fourteenth century: *forte, grande, gentile, tele*. Note, however, that in fixed expressions with *grand* the *e* was never added: *grand'chose, grand'mère*. The apostrophe was introduced by later grammarians as an indication that they perceived the lack of an *e*, although they did not pronounce it. The plural pronoun *il* became *ilz* or *ils* at this time; the feminine possessive pronoun *moie* gave way to a form *mienne*, copied from the masculine *mien*. The possessive *leur* was no longer invariable.

In the verb forms there was a marked leveling by analogy. The verb *aimer* came to be conjugated as it is today instead of *aim, aimes, aime, amons, amez, aiment*. Similarly *trouver* lost its forms *truis* and *treuve* and conformed throughout to *trouver*. Levelings such as these were not always consistently adhered to as yet. The conditional and imperfect terminations *–oie, –oies, –oit* tended to become *–ois, –ois, –oit*, pronounced as though written *ais*, etc. The vowel *e* spread throughout the subjunctive present endings: *je chante*, not *je chant; tu chantes*, not *tu chanz*. There were numerous other alterations which cannot be classified generally, such as *sui > suis, criembre > craindre*.

37 B. STUDY OF FRENCH

It is true that in the thirteenth century such grammatical treatises as the *Petit traité de conjugaisons françaises* [4] and Gautier de Bibbesworth's *Pour apprendre le français* had come into existence, but such handbooks for the teaching of French to foreigners, usually to Englishmen, were not extensively used before the Middle French period.[5]

In the last quarter of the thirteenth century an alphabetical lexicon of Latin words defined in French appeared. This is referred to as the *Abavus*, since that is the first word in the list. Derivatives of the lexicon were very popular in the fourteenth century. See Mario Roques' *Recueil général des lexiques français du moyen-âge* (Paris, 1936–   ), I. The *Abavus* may be called the first dictionary in which French was used, although it is not, of course, a French dictionary.

For information on the French element in English, in the fourteenth century, consult J. Mersand, *Chaucer's Romance Vocabulary*.[6]

38. TRANSLATION

Toutesvoies pour avoir ouy bruit et rumeur qui se menoit dessoubz

---

[4] Cambridge MS. Trinity R. 3. 56.

[5] Consult an article by Stengel in *ZfrS.*, I, 1 ff., who publishes some of them; also J. Gessler, *La maniere de langage* (Paris: Droz, 1935).

[6] Comet Press Inc., 1937.

la maistre cabine et qui sembloit que ce fust celluy qui peusce provenir de aulcune beste tressauvage qui voulsist s'embler, si doncques feïmes resolution d'enquerir la cause d'icelluy.   De ce advient que trouvames Eumoulpe assis devant un grant parchemin et qui escripvoit diverses histoires en vers, dont fusmes esbahis que loisir lui fust de rimer quant la mort tresperilleuse et puante nous attaingnoit.   En cest endroict le boutames avant qui crioit et pleuroit et luy ordonnames d'estre raisonable, mais cestuy fut si irascu et si actaint de desplaisance qu'il dist: « Laissiez que je finisce mes vers, lor fin n'est pas chose legiere. » Moy, je le contraignis le fol paillart et je priai a Dione de l'estendre groignant sur la terre.

We attempt to reproduce our original passage here in the language of 1450.   Note that the syntax is more clumsy than in our translation of Chapter III.   The Latinized spellings and the frequency of correlative expressions should also be remarked: e.g., *bruit et rumeur, tresperilleuse et puante,* etc.

REFERENCES

As in the previous chapter, and

CHATELAIN, HENRI, *Recherches sur le vers français au quinzième siècle* (Paris: Champion, 1908).

VI

THE HUMANISTIC RENAISSANCE

(1494–1610)

39. GENERAL CONDITIONS

The term " Renaissance," when used in the history of civilization, means that a large mass of people have changed their point of view — their outlook on life and its surrounding conditions. We have seen how the Middle Ages, with all their fineness of faith and enthusiasm, wore themselves out in the Middle French period; the people reacted and demanded something new. The novelty which presented itself ready to hand was the pseudo-pagan civilization of Italy. Italy had never been suited to medieval institutions. During the eleventh, twelfth, and thirteenth centuries she attempted to combine a hodgepodge of art and literature from France, Germany, the Arabs, the Lombards, Byzantium, and antiquity; but from Dante's time (1265–1321) forward she recovered and, casting off foreign influence, set herself to reviving ancient art and letters. Her success was admirable. Italian architecture, sculpture, and painting made remarkable strides at once. In literature such masters as Dante, Petrarch, and Boccaccio not only cultivated Latin literature to a high degree; they gave Florence — and therefore Italy — a vernacular literature which was far in advance of any existing elsewhere in Europe. They dignified and tended to fix the Italian language. They were succeeded by a flood of humanists in both Latin and Italian.[1]

A scanty conception of Greek, in the Middle Ages, was derived from Donatus, Priscian, Isidore, and Roger Bacon. In the fifteenth century, thanks to the Council at Florence (1439) where the hierarchy of the Roman and Greek churches sought in vain for unity, Greek language and literature come to the fore. One of the Greek

---

[1] We should define a humanist as a man of critical mind whose chief interest is the history of civilization and letters, which he pursues for no practical consideration. Commonly this interest is in ancient civilization; such was the case in the sixteenth century.

bishops, Bessarion, joined the Church of Rome and was made a cardinal. He was inspired with a love of Plato's writings and he encouraged the study of Greek and of Plato at Florence. With the Fall of Constantinople in 1453 still further immigrations into Italy were made by Byzantine scholars with their precious Greek MSS. John Lascaris (1445–1535) became a teacher of the Greek language and wrote a grammar that was used as a model thereafter. The Medici family at Florence encouraged this humanism to a high degree.

Suddenly the French people, bankrupt spiritually as they were, were made aware of Italian humanism by the Italian Wars (1494–1525), when thousands of Frenchmen visited Naples, Milan, and other cities en route. The city of Lyons had always been an open door to some influence from Italy; it now became a veritable and wide-open floodgate.[2] All of this was favored by the discovery of the use of movable type which we speak of as the invention of printing (1434). Presumably the discoverer was Johann Gutenberg (1400–1468), who began first at Strassburg and who was at Mainz in 1448. His first great book was the forty-two line Bible which was printed between 1450 and 1455. In 1470 printing was introduced into France by Ulrich Gering, Michael Freyburger, and Martin Krantz, who printed for some three years in the Sorbonne building; later they moved around the corner to a location on the Rue Saint-Jacques. But books were still expensive and the common people could not buy them. It was the Venetian printer Aldus Manutius (1449–1515) who led the movement to make books cheaper. His printing house was founded in 1490.

As a result of the new age of reason which was flourishing religious doctrine was ripe for a reform. Although men such as Wycliffe, Huss, and others had made a brief stir in previous centuries, it was Martin Luther (1483–1546), a German monk, who shook the Catholic world in 1519–1521. A still more evangelical protestantism was preached by the Frenchman Jean Calvin (1509–1564), of whom we shall say more presently. France was torn asunder by the forces of Calvin and those of the Catholic Church in intermittent warfare during the sixteenth century.

In the Middle Ages education was almost entirely under the direction of the Church. (When we make an exception we are thinking of the *jongleurs* schools.) With the founding of the *Collège*

---

[2] Certain French critics of the present day wish to minimize this Italian influence. See Leon Wiley in *Stud. in Phil.*, XXXIV, 248–59.

Royal (1530) under the direction of Guillaume Budé we greet secular education! At first the French humanists welcomed Protestantism, but soon they saw that Protestant theology was vastly more narrow than that which the traditional Church had taught; and so you find a series of humanists at this time, some avowedly Protestant and others Catholic, but all tending towards free thought. We have in mind Rabelais, Montaigne, and the Estiennes.

Much as they admired the Latin and Greek languages sensible men realized fully that their language was French, and they saw that a lasting reform of letters must take this fact into account. All the humanists spoke and wrote Latin with great ease, but they knew that they could make no impression upon the people at large as long as they used a foreign tongue. So we find these " Latinists " undertaking to dignify the French language, and to remove it from a " degradation " which they referred to contemptuously as *gothique*. Propaganda was dear to the men of this century. Since, in their estimation, there was no literature in the French language worthy of the name, it was necessary to remove this deficiency by translations. Since the grammar tended to be non-existent they wished to make one. Since the French vocabulary seemed to them inelegant, and to some the spelling appeared barbarous, these reforms were also put on the calendar.

40. THE TRANSLATORS AND FRENCH PROSE WRITERS

In the forefront of humanistic translators we place a Savoyard, Claude de Seyssel (1450–1520), who translated Xenophon, Diodorus Siculus, Thucydides, Seneca, Appian, Justin, and Rufinus, into French. This Seyssel was an intimate friend of John Lascaris; most of his translating was for Louis XII (1498–1515). Seyssel was particularly haunted by the lack of a *licterature en françois*, for he did not consider the *Tristans, Girons, et Lancelots* which already existed, worthy of such a name.[3] Seyssel was bishop of Marseilles and later archbishop of Turin. It is certain that his influence was within a limited circle because his translations were not published till much later. Jean Lemaire de Belges praised the French language as a literary medium in his *Concorde des deux langages* (meaning Italian and French), but Geoffroy Tory (d. 1534) deserves the credit for being one of the very first to emphasize in print the value of French, in his *Champ Fleury* (1529):

[3] See prologue to his translation of Justin, made in 1509, but printed in 1557.

Il me semble soubz correction quil seroit plus beau a ung Francois
escripre en francois quen autre langage, tant pour la seurete de son dict
langage Francois, que pour decorer sa Nation & enrichir sa langue do-
mestique, qui est aussi belle & bonne que une autre, quant elle est bien
couchee par escript (12 r.) . . . Sil est vray que toutes choses ont eu com-
mancement, il est certain que la langue Grecque, semblablement la Latine
ont este quelque temps incultes & sans Reigle de Grammaire, comme est
de present la nostre (4 v.) . . . Ie scay quil ya mains bons esperits . . .
pensant que langue Francoise ne soit pas assez bonne ny elegante.   Saulve
leur honneur elle est une des plusbelles & gracieuses de toutes les langues
humaines . . . (24 r.).

So popular did translating activity become that in 1540 Etienne
Dolet — of whom more later — published his *Manière de bien traduire
d'une langue dans l'autre.*   The greatest of the early translators was
Jacques Amyot (1513–1593), bishop of Auxerre, whom we designate
as the earliest stylist of the French language.   By his logical well-
balanced sentence structure, he began that reform of French syntax
which was so much needed.   He rendered into French the works of
Diodorus Siculus, *Daphnis and Chlœ*, and above all, Plutarch's
Lives:

Vous aurez pour agreable l'humble affection que j'ai eue en ce faisant,
de recommander a la posterité la memoire de votre glorieux regne, de
servir au bien public de vos sujets et d'enrichir notre langue françoise,
selon la faible portee de mon peu de sens et de litterature . . . (Preface to
translation of Plutarch, addressed to King Henry II of France).

We must consider as a translator the French religious reformer
Jean Cauvin, whose name was later Latinized to Calvinus and thence
became French once more as Calvin.   His *Institutio religionis chris-
tianae* was issued first in Latin in 1536 and, translated by him into
French, published at Strassburg in 1541.   A revised Latin edition
was printed in 1559 and translated into French by the following
year.   Calvin marks a great advance in style and balance of syntax
over Amyot, who was his contemporary; in fact, it is most interesting to compare Calvin's French style of 1541 with his own revision
of 1560.   There is notable progress in language.

When we speak of these translators we have in mind those who
used the French language with reverence, with the express purpose
of making it richer.   There existed, of course, fragmentary adapta-
tions of the Bible into French since the early Middle Ages.   In the
sixteenth century we meet the French New Testament of Lefèvre
d'Etaples [4] inspired by the German Luther Bible, and the *Bible de*

---

[4] Paris: Simon de Colines, 1523.

Serrières completed by Calvin's cousin Olivétan in 1535. These versions had no particular literary merit and were utilitarian in intent. Similarly there were hosts of minor works on arithmetic and other practical matters, naturally couched in French, for the simple folk. These do not form a part of our story of the embellishment of the French language. Works in surgery began to be translated after 1530; the naturalists Ruel, Pierre Belon, and Guillaume Rondelet encouraged the spread of their works in French as well as in Latin. Bernard Palissy (1510–1589) wrote his *Discours admirables*[5] and Ambroise Paré his *Œuvres* (1561) in French, but these men were not learned and *could* not write in Latin.

The greatest victory for the French language was in sections 110 and 111 of the royal edict of Villers-Cotterets (1539), which demanded that French alone be used in all courts and in all judicial acts. In 1579 Henri Estienne (1528–1598), the celebrated scholar and printer, issued his *Precellence du langage françois.*

The men whom we have cited thus far as defenders of the French language in prose have been ecclesiastics, printers, and scientists. Of similarly great influence were the *noblesse de robe* — the lawyers and *présidents.* After the edict of Villers-Cotterets they were definitely won over to the use of French in place of Latin. These men are our earliest historians of medieval history and vernacular literature. Such an individual as Etienne Pasquier (1529–1615), although his great *Recherches de la France* appeared posthumously, must have had immerse influence. Claude Fauchet (1530–1601), our first chronicler of Old French literature, wrote after 1579, inspired by his perusal of old MSS.[6] Jean de Nostredame (1507– ?), another lawyer, was the author of a *Vies des plus célèbres et anciens poètes provençaux* (1575) in the vernacular. The authority of such gentlemen of the robe in matters of French language and literature seemed so well established at the close of the sixteenth century that it was a moot question whether their usage, since a standard was now sought, should not be taken as the best in France.

41. THE POETIC MOVEMENTS

The *Rhétoriqueurs* of the early sixteenth century made no contribution to the French language, unless we count obscurity as one.

---

[5] Paris: Martin le Jeune, 1580.

[6] We mention in particular his *Recueil de l'origine de la langue et poesie françoise* (Paris: Mamert Patisson, 1581).

The son of one of them — the graceful Clément Marot (1497–1544) — has more to his credit. Throughout the Middle Ages French writers were in doubt whether to make the past participle agree with an object in such compound expressions as *j'ai veu la dame*. Should one say *j'ai veue la dame?* Supposedly Marot settled this controversy with his *Epigramme LXXVII:*

Enfans, oyez une lecon:
Nostre langue a ceste façon
Que le terme qui va devant
Voluntiers regist le suyvant.
Les vieux exemples je suyvray
Pour le mieulx: car, a dire vray,
La chanson fut bien ordonnee
Qui dit: *M'amour vous ay donnee,*
Voila la force que possede
Le femenin, quand il precede.

Or prouveray par bons tesmoings
Que tous pluriers n'en font pas moins;
Il faut dire en termes parfaictz:
Dieu en ce monde nous a faictz. . . .
L'italien, dont la faconde
Passe les vulgaires du monde,
Son langage a ainsi basty. . . .

This is the rule of participle agreement as we have it today. It is nonetheless true that Marot's dictum would not have survived had it not been supported by grammarians in the seventeenth century. Note also that Marot names Italian as the queen of all the vernacular languages and names it as a model.

This worship of Italian was being strongly emphasized by a movement under way in Italy. Cardinal Peter Bembo (1470–1547) was the leader. One of Bembo's disciples, Sperone Speroni, published a small volume of *Dialoghi*[7] which included a *Dialogo delle lingue* in defense of Italian, beside Latin, as a literary medium. This little volume was so popular that it was frequently reprinted.

Peletier du Mans (1517–1582) was a strange mixture of poet and mathematician. Although he wrote learnedly in Latin on the circle and tangent angles, yet he saw the necessity for enriching the French language with works of this sort: " Pansez quele immortalite eles pourroet aporter a une langue " (*Dialogue d'orthographe*, bk. 2).

---

[7] Venice: Aldus, 1542.

It is more than probable that these same ideas on enrichment of the vernacular were his as early as 1543 when he was intimate with Ronsard. The influence of Peletier on the young Ronsard is now accepted by the critics. With the theories of Peletier ringing in their ears, with the dialogue of Sperone Speroni before them, Ronsard (1524–1585) and Du Bellay (1522–1560) planned their *Deffense et Illustration de la Langue francoyse*,[8] of which the actual text was written by Du Bellay. This brief prose work saw eleven editions between 1549 and 1597; it was not again reprinted until 1839. The linguistic program of Ronsard was further presented in his *Préface des odes* (1550), *Abrégé de l'art poétique* (1565), *Première préface de la Franciade* (1572), and *Deuxième préface de la Franciade* (posthumous, 1585). Compare also the prefaces by Du Bellay: *Préface des vers lyriques* (1549), *Préface de l'Olive* (1550), and *Epître au Seigneur de Morel* (1552). As we should expect, these theories were supported by Peletier du Mans in his *L'art poétique départi en deux livres*.[9] Hostility was expressed in the *Quintil Horatian* (1550), which has long been attributed to Charles Fontaine; but Barthélemy Aneau has also been suggested as the author.

We shall present the doctrine of Ronsard and his school, not confining ourselves exclusively to the contents of the *Deffense*. They wished to maintain the value of the French language against the pedants who preferred Latin, and against the ignorant who were corrupting their native French. Since a great language, in their estimation, always possessed more words than an unembellished tongue they proposed to increase the French vocabulary. They encouraged the following methods:

(1) *Ne crains donc poëte futur, d'innover quelques termes . . . (Deff.* II, 6) — that is, do not be afraid to coin new words; (2) borrow moderately from the ancient languages: *Se compose donc, qui voudra enrichir sa langue, a l'imitation des meilleurs auteurs grecs et latins . . . Mais . . . Je t'admoneste donc . . . de non imiter a pied levé (Deff.* I, 8). Also Ronsard said: *Tu composeras hardiment des mots a l'imitation des Grecs et Latins (Art Poét.)*; (3) borrow dialect words: *Tu sauras dextrement choisir et approprier a ton œuvre les mots plus significatifs des dialectes de notre France . . . (Art Poét.)*; (4) borrow words from the trades and jargons: *Encore te veux-je avertir de hanter quelquefois . . . toutes sortes d'ouvriers et gens mecaniques (Deff.*

---

[8] Paris: Arnoul l'Angelier, 1549. The best edition today is that of Henri Chamard (Paris: Fontemoing, 1904).

[9] Lyon: Jean de Tournes et Guillaume Gazeau, 1555.

II, 11); (5) revive old words by new formations: *De tous vocables
... en usage ou hors d'usage, s'il reste encore quelque partie d'eux,
tu le pourras par bonne et certaine analogie faire croitre et multiplier
... (Art Poét.)*.

They also made suggestions for metrical usage: (1) use of cæsura
after fourth or sixth syllable: (2) use of *enjambement;* (3) do not
count metrically the mute *e* in such a word as *espées* in the middle
of a line; count the *espées* as though written *espés;* (4) alternate
masculine and feminine rhymes; (5) rich rhymes are preferable.
They also recommended that all the types of poetry present in
Greek and Latin literature, such as the ode, long didactic poem,
and so on, be represented in French.   Ronsard contributed a national epic with his *Franciade*.[10]

Before Ronsard and Du Bellay ended their poetic careers they
tacitly changed their minds with regard to some of their more
extreme suggestions — chief among these being their theory of
coining and making new derivations.   Many of the post-Pléiade
poets, those who flourished between 1570 and 1600, did not perceive
this subtle change on the part of their master Ronsard.   Such
maladept poetasters as Edouard du Monin and Christophle Gamon
ruined Ronsard's taste for poetry, by his own avowal.   Guillaume de
Salluste, Sieur du Bartas (1544–1590), was included by Ronsard in
the list of his unworthy imitators, but in this Ronsard was exces-
sively severe.   It is true that Du Bartas went the early Ronsard
one better in such new poetic forms as *ba-battant, sou-soufflant,* and
ciel porte-tonnerre, etc., but it must be remembered that Du Bartas
later heeded the counsel of those who had taste and reduced the
number of these absurdities himself.   Du Bartas was anxious to
obey the injunctions of the *Deffense et Illustration*, which demanded a
long didactic poem in the French language, when he wrote his *Pre-
miere* and *Seconde Sepmaines*.   Philippe Desportes (1546–1606) was
one of the few post-Pléiade poets who felt the need for moderation
in vocabulary.   He was strongly influenced by the Italians and made
use of many antitheses and bizarre similes, but he never neglected
clarity.   Despite such efforts he was the poet particularly chosen for
correction by Malherbe, as we shall see in the following chapter.
What would Malherbe have done if he had sought to comment upon
the earlier works of Du Bartas ?

[10] Incomplete in 1572.

42. DICTIONARIES

In the Old and Middle French period there were no French dictionaries as we understand the term. Latin MSS. sometimes had comments and translation helps in the margin; there were also a few word lists such as the *De utensilibus* of Alexander Neckam, which gave the Latin names of utensils used about the household, and the *Abavus* (§ 37 B). But an alphabetical list of the French vocabulary which could be consulted as a norm for the spelling and meaning of French words did not exist before the *Dictionaire Francoislatin* of Robert Estienne (1503–1559) the printer, father of Henri Estienne.[11]   In 1549 Estienne issued a second version of his *Dictionaire Francoislatin* with additions and improvements which was to be the standard for the following fifty years. After Robert's death other reprintings with further additions were issued in 1564, 1572, and 1584.   In 1606 this same dictionary served as the basis for Jean Nicot's *Thrésor de la langue françoyse* [12] in which the French words were for the first time defined in French as well as in Latin. This work by Nicot did not meet with much favor.   The French-Latin form was preferred to the " all French " and a reduction into smaller size of Estienne's work was reprinted as late as 1628 under the title *Grand dictionnaire françois-latin*.

We are not much concerned here with Latin-French and various types of polyglot dictionaries.   These do not concern French lexicography as much as they do Latin. Chief among such works was the *Dictionarium* of Ambrosius Calepinus, an Italian monk, which first appeared at Reggio, Italy, in 1503.   At first the dictionary was entirely in Latin, but after 1575 definitions were added in four, eight, nine, ten, and even eleven languages.   The edition of Basel (1590) contained equivalents in Hebrew, Greek, French, Italian, German, Spanish, English, Dutch, Aramaic, Polish, and Hungarian. It is indicative of the character of the age that the people should think of Calepin, when they had a dictionary in mind, rather than of the sober and more useful work by Estienne.   The word *calepin* passed into everyday speech for notebook or handbook of any kind. Here is an example from the *Mitistoire baragouine* (1549) of Guillaume des Autels: " *Elle lui tira son calepin d'injures,*" and the

---

[11] The first edition of this, in 1539, was merely a rearrangement of Robert Estienne's *Dictionarium Latino-Gallicum* (1538) which had very little value for French lexicography since it was a list of Latin words with French meaning.
[12] Paris: David Douceur.

lady then proceeds to swear at the gentleman in a list of insults arranged in alphabetical order until she reaches the letter *d*, when the gentleman takes a stick!

43. SPELLING

The system of orthography used by Robert Estienne was that of the law practitioners and we have observed the absurdities of this etymological spelling in a previous chapter. Thus Estienne contributed to the permanence of this fantastic spelling. There were many complaints, but it was Louis Meigret (1517–1582) who made the first definite contribution to the subject. He had reflected on the matter as early as 1530; but it was in 1542 that he published his first attack: *Traité touchant le commun usage de l'escriture Françoise*. He followed this with a model of his own system in *Le menteur, ou incredule de Lucian traduit de Grẹc en Frãçoẹs* [13]. He was opposed particularly by Guillaume des Autels and Peletier du Mans, and this meant a succession of pamphlets on the subject passing back and forth. Des Autels used the pseudonym of Glaomalis de Vezelet in his attacks. Briefly, Meigret's system was as follows: (1) Suppress all the superfluous letters such as *g, t, d, l, n, s, c, p, u* which are not pronounced, as in *ung, et, renards, aultre, ayment, beste, dict, escripvre*, and *que* which Meigret would write *un, ẹ, renars, aotre, aymet, bẹte, dit, ecrire*, and *qe;* (2) write *ẹ* for *ai* as in *parfait, o* for *u* as in *unde, o* for *ou* as in *pouvoir, ao* for *au* as in *autre, oẹ* for *oy* as in *roy*, and *j* for *ge* in such an orthographic spelling as *gageons* (1st pl. of *gager);* (3) use *z* for *s* where *s* is so pronounced as in *chose, ç* not *t* in *manifestation, x* for *ct* in *diction, s* for *z* in *aymez, bontez*, and *aos* for *aux* in such plurals as *chevaux;* (4) palatal *ill* should be represented by *ll'* in such words as *meilleur*. We now give a specimen of Meigret's reform spelling:

Qẹlle rezon sarions nous mẹttr'en avant pour couurir cete grande betize …? Tẹllemēt qe tout einsi qe je m'efforçe de decharjer notr'ecritture dẹ' lettres superflúes, ẹ la rendre lizable suivant l'uzaje de la prolacíọn: çeus la ao contrére ne luy pẹnsent pas fẹre peu d'honeur ẹn la parãt de plumes d'aotruy pour la degyzer. ...

This passage is drawn from Meigret's *Reponse a la dezesperee replique de Glaomalis de Vezelet* (1551). Observe his inconsistency in not writing *pẹnset* for *pẹnsent*. Strange to relate, Meigret did not

[13] Paris: Wechel, 1548.

discontinue the use of *y* for *i*, nor did he suggest distinction of *u* and *v*.

The great Ronsard was impressed by Meigret and the result was a slightly reformed spelling used by the French poets in the third quarter of the sixteenth century. Ronsard adopted *z* for *s* in such words as *chose*, he preferred the consonantal *i* (that is *j*) in the place of *ge*, and he suppressed many of the superfluous consonants. He went Meigret one better in opposing the use of *y* for *i;* he also abolished *ph* in favor of *f* in such words as *philosophe*. But Ronsard did not abide by these reforms after 1565. There is speculation as to whether he was dissuaded by Du Bellay or whether Amadis Jamyn, Ronsard's secretary, substituted the traditional spelling in the poems that he copied for the press. Meigret had abandoned his own reform even earlier. He wrote in 1554: *Si le bastiment de l'escripture vous semble autre et different de la doctrine qu'autrefois ie mis en avant, blamez en l' imprimeur qui a préferé son gain à la raison* ... (*Discours touchant la création du monde*).

Pierre de la Ramée (1515–1572), or Ramus in Latinized form, is always remembered today because he emphasized in his *Gramere* (1562) the distinction between *i* and *j*, *u* and *v*. For his full system it is necessary to consult the second edition of the *Gramere* (1572). There we find *e* for *au*, *ad* for *eu*, 8 for *ou*, ç for *ch*,] for palatal *l*, ɔ for *gn*, as well as the *j* and *v*. This system by Ramus attracted very little attention. The so-called *lettres ramistes* (*j* and *v*) were adopted first in the Low Countries and spread from there back to France. A schoolmaster of Marseilles, one Honorat Rambaud, suggested the use of an entirely new alphabet in his *La Declaration des abus que lon commet en escrivant*.[14] This fantastic suggestion was never seriously considered. The fever for spelling reform quieted down towards the end of the century. A few of the post-Pléiade poets continued some of the modifications of Ronsard; but Pasquier was able to remark in his *Recherches de la France* at the end of the century that the efforts towards spelling reform had come to a quiet end (VIII, ch. I).

44. ACCENTS AND PUNCTUATION

The history of our punctuation marks has never been adequately treated. Presumably the schoolmasters at Alexandria, whom we refer to collectively as *scholiasts*, devised such marks for the Greek

[14] Lyon: Jean de Tournes, 1578.

language in the second century B.C. These were the period, comma, semicolon (used as a question mark), and a dot resembling the upper part of a colon. The Latins began to use some of these in the fourth century A.D., but they did not find favor. Donatus, Cassiodorus [15] and Isidore of Seville transmitted knowledge of these punctuation signs to the scribes who devised the Carolingian minuscule manuscript hand during the middle of Charlemagne's reign (c. 790 A.D.). The Carolingian scribes wished to express three things: a full stop for which they used ⁊ or ⁊̇ or · or —⁊̇; a half stop which they expressed by . or /; and the question mark for which they used ꝰ. These marks were almost entirely neglected in France after a few centuries. By the thirteenth century in France many scribes used no punctuation marks except ⸗ for a hyphen. A few continued the use of the period and of a stroke / meaning a half stop. In Italy, during the fourteenth century, the half stop / came to resemble the modern colon (:). The Gutenberg Bible (1450-1455) used the hyphen ⸗, the period, the stop resembling a colon, a question mark (¿) and the point high on the line (·). The edition of Villon published by Levet at Paris in 1489 had no punctuation marks whatsoever, save an occasional colon.

It was Aldus Manutius of Venice who began regularly to use what we should call today the comma, semicolon, colon, and the question mark right-side-up. Obviously his ? is the same as Gutenberg's ¿ and the Carolingian ꝰ. Aldus's semicolon is probably derived from the Carolingian ⁊̇ rather than directly from the Greek; he used also the (;.) as a full stop, which resembles a Carolingian device. The French printers of the sixteenth century continued to print only the period, the colon, the upper point, and the /, until Geoffroy Tory led the way in 1525. He introduced the comma into French texts. Slowly the / disappeared.

The story of the accents is somewhat parallel to this. The same Alexandrine scholiasts devised a system of ten accentual marks for the Greek language, in the second century B.C. These were the acute accent (´), the grave (`), the circumflex (^), the apostrophe, the long mark (¯), the short mark (˘), the hyphen, the separator sign (,), and the rough and smooth breathing marks. These became known to the Latins in the fourth century A.D., but they did virtually nothing with them. Even the Carolingian scribes of Charlemagne's era found no use for them, except for the acute accent. During the remainder of the Middle Ages the only accent mark used

[15] Cf. Migne, *Patrol. Latina*, LXX, 1130.

in French and Latin MSS. was the stroke over an *i*, resembling an acute accent but longer, which was used first to distinguish a double *i* from an *n* or a *u;* later it was used over a single *i* and in the fifteenth-century Italian hand it became what is today: a dot over the *i*. It was again Aldus Manutius, the Venetian printer, who adopted the Greek accents for Latin use early in the sixteenth century. He explained them fully in his *Institutiones grammaticae* (1508; and many editions thereafter). The printers at Lyons may have been the first to adopt these accents for Latin texts printed in France. In any case, it was Geoffroy Tory who first furthered their spread with his Latin *Heures a l'usage de Rome* (1525).

In his *Champ Fleury* (1529) Tory expressed the need for accents in French:

En ce passage daccent, nous avons imperfection a la quelle nous doibrions remedier en purifiant e mettant a Reigle & Art certain nostre langue qui est la plus gracieuse quon sache (fol. 52 r.); Je dis & allegue ces choses icy ... on ... porroit escripre ung point crochu qui signifie quil y a quelque Vocale ou le S ostez ... (fol. 56 v.).

This last suggests the use of the apostrophe. The following year (1530) Robert Estienne employed the acute accent on the past participles such as *aimé, donné,* in an edition of the *De corrupti sermonis* of Mathurin Cordier. Tory was the first to use the *c* cedilla in French in a book entitled *Le sacre et coronnement de la Royne* (1530 old style). This device had been used by Spanish printers since 1488. In the *Adolescence Clementine* of Clement Marot which Tory printed in 1533, he employed an apostrophe, placing it in three positions to indicate apostrophe, acute accent, and cedilla. The first treatise on accentuation was the *Briefve doctrine* (1533) of an otherwise unknown Montflory. This work was eclipsed in popularity by the Lyonese printer Etienne Dolet (1509–1546) with his *La maniere de bien traduire d'une langue en aultre, d'avantage de la punctuation de la langue francoyse, plus des accents d'yselle.*[16] Dolet's book remained the standard reference throughout the sixteenth century.

45. GRAMMARS

The honor of writing the first worthy grammar of the French language belongs to an Englishman, John Palsgrave (d. 1554). His

[16] Lyons: Dolet, 1540.

L'Esclarcissement de la langue françoyse (1532),[17] written in English despite the title, was the first attempt to subject the language to the restrictions of artificial grammar. As a specimen we quote some of the paradigm of the verb " to be ":

Whose Complet Conjugation Here Immediately Foloweth. Je suys, tu es, il est, nous sómmes, vous éstez, ilz sont. I am. Jestóye, tu estóys, il estóyt, nous estións, vous estiéz, ils estóyent. I was.

There were three books or divisions to this work, but the third does little more than re-emphasize the second. We must not forget another French grammar written in England for Princess Mary. This was the *Introductorie for to lerne to rede, to pronounce, and to speke French trewly* by the Frenchman Gilles du Wez, a rival to Palsgrave. The date of this is 1532 also, but it is not equal to the other.

Jacques Dubois (1478–1555), a physician who Latinized his name to J. Silvius Ambianus, was the first Frenchman to prepare a grammar for use in France. This was his *In linguam gallicam Isagoge*.[18] Unfortunately the plan of this book was not useful. Dubois did not attempt to fix the language as it was. Convinced that French was bad Latin, he wished to improve French with the aid of Latin. The spelling reformer Louis Meigret also tried his hand at grammar at the press of Chrestien Wechsel (Paris, 1550). He omitted syntax entirely and devoted his effort to morphology and etymology. Of this last he was pitifully ignorant. He had some idea of good and bad usage, however, and he invoked nature, rather than Latin, as his authority. Livet calls Meigret the founder of modern French grammar. The *Traicté de la grammaire francoise* (1557) of Robert Estienne was beautifully printed, but it was incomplete and founded too closely upon Dubois and Meigret. Next is the *Gramere* (1562 and second edition, 1572) of Pierre Ramus. Here there is a distinction between morphology (called etymology) and syntax; but much of the material was borrowed from Meigret. Ramus was more concerned with method than with subject matter. He wished to discard completely the old systems of grammatical classification of the Latin grammarians Priscian and Donat. Apparently Ramus was the first to suggest the usage of people at the king's court as superior to other brands of French, but he did little

---

[17] A modern reprint is in the *Documents inédits sur l'histoire de France*, with the date 1852.

[18] Paris: Robert Estienne, 1531.

more than make this suggestion. Henri Estienne reprinted his father's grammar in 1582 and added to it his own *Hypomneses de gallica lingua.* In this his remarks on the syntax of the pronouns, on the position of attributive adjectives, and on the article were the best pages of grammar that had appeared so far. Other grammars were by Etienne Pasquier (1572), Beza (1584), Tabourot (1587), and Lanoue (1596), but these added nothing of importance. We might have mentioned also in more detail the grammars by Jean Pillot (1550), and Antoine Cauchie (1570), but it would have been only because of their early date; they had very little value.

46. VOCABULARY

The suggestions by sixteenth century humanists and poets that the vocabulary be increased have been traced in our preceding sections. No statistics on the actual number of new words and on their respective sources can be satisfactory before the publication of the dictionary by Huguet which we have listed at the close of the chapter. The first French writer to expand his vocabulary in a remarkable way was the great François Rabelais (d. 1553) who began writing in 1532. In the two volumes by L. Sainéan entitled *La langue de Rabelais* [19] some 3,770 words are discussed, which might give some idea of the innovations and borrowings by Rabelais. No other writer or poet of the sixteenth century approached Rabelais in the exploitation of new vocabulary. It is worthy of note that Rabelais himself mocked the habit of turning too many learned Latin words into French. In *Pantagruel,* ch. 6, the hero takes a stroll at the gate of Orleans and meets a Limousin scholar who is coming from Paris. On being questioned the Limousin replies in a language of which we give a specimen:

> Nous tranfretons la Séquane au dilucule et crepuscule, nous deambulons par les compites et quadrivies de l'urbe ... puis cauponizons es tabernes meritoires ... belles spatules vervecines performaminees de petrosil. ...

This sort of *escorche-Latin* could not have been infrequent among the humanists of Rabelais's day.

As we should expect, the other source for much borrowing was from the Italian. Henri Estienne ridiculed the habit of using too many Italian words in French speech in his *Deux dialogues du nouveau langage françois italianizé* (1578). We give a specimen:

[19] Paris: Boccard, 1923.

Philausone. Bon jour a vostre seigneurie, monsieur Celtophile. Puis qu'elle s'allegre tant de m'avoir rencontré, je jouiray d'une allegresse reciproque de m'etre imbatu en ce lieu. Mais il plaira a vostre seigneurie piller patience si je luy di qu'elle a usé en mon endroit d'une façon de langage qui n'a point bon garbe.

Spanish furnished some new words, particularly towards the close of the sixteenth century such as *fanfarre, diane, cassolette, escamoter, habler*, etc., but these were apt to be military words or expressions used in derision, because they were acquired mostly through combat with the Spaniards in the Low Countries and elsewhere.

Suffice it to say that in accord with the plan of the humanists and of the poets, the French language acquired a vast conglomeration of new words at this time — so large that we need a special dictionary such as that of Huguet, or Cotgrave, to understand them. Although the Pléiade, on second thought, countenanced moderation, it remained for the purists of the following era to bring order out of this chaos.

47. SYNTAX

We have mentioned that the writers of the century, particularly Amyot and Calvin, sought more logic and clarity in their sentence structure. The subject pronouns and the article came to be used more regularly. The partitive construction with *des* supplanted the plural *uns* in such as *j'ai des amis*. The reflexive of the verb came to be used more in place of a passive construction; *qui* replaced *que* entirely as a subject pronoun. The use of *soy* in such formations as *pour soy former* gave way to *se;* but the personal pronouns *luy*, etc., also tended to replace the reflexive altogether.

48. MORPHOLOGY

Such forms as *ou* < *en le* and *es* < *en les* gradually fell into disuse. Such demonstratives as *cestui, iceluy*, and *cil* went out of current use. The *s* became regular in the first person singular, present indicative, of the *–ir* and *–re* conjugations, as well in such verbs as *je voi–s;* cf. *je dis, je vends*. The imperfect subjunctive *–issions, –issiez* endings gave way to the more regular *–assions, –assiez*.

49. PRONUNCIATION

The *r* between vowels had become so weak, beginning thus in the Middle Ages, that it came to be confused with a *z* sound (spelled *s*).

For instance *Paris* and *Pasis*, *chaire* and *chaise*, *bericles* and *besicles*, *courin* and *cousin* were similar in popular speech. Note that we preserve today a form *chaise* beside *chaire*, also *bésicles* instead of *béricles*. In these last two cases the forms with *s* had no right to existence and are simply due to this confusion. Such a combination as *eau* was doubtless pronounced *iau* at the beginning of the sixteenth century; within a hundred years it was reduced to its modern sound. The mute *e* within the interior of words began to disappear: *surplis* < *surpelis*, *bourlet* < *bourrelet*. The *oi* continued to have the pronunciations [we] and [e] and in some words was still *oi*. The sound [wa], if it existed, was confined to low people. Consonants continued to be pronounced at the end of a word before a pause or before a vowel, but **not** before a consonant. The *x* was pronounced as *s* or *z:* as in **examples** where it had the sound of *z*.

50. TRANSLATION

I. Early sixteenth century (in the manner of Rabelais):

A tant ouyrent dans l'officine majeure esclandre horrificque, lequel cuyderent issir de quelque beste sauvage voulant eschapper fors. Ainsi se mirent en deliberation d'en chercher curieusement la cause, dont se fist que trouvames Eumolpe deuant un grand parchemin, matagrabolisant chronicques et les reduisant en carmes. Et fusmes merueilleusement esbaubis de la contenance d'icelluy, qui cuydoit loisir luy estre de rimer, soy veant en bel estat de rendre l'anme. Adoncs, le trouvant en telle obstination, le boutasmes avant a proufict de mesnaige luy menant bruyt comme cinq cent pannerees de deables de Vanvert, et luy ordonnasmes de retourner a la raison. Mais ce paillard estoit si tellement tabusté de son entendement qu'il disoit: « Laissez-moy que je finisse ces vers, la fin d'iceulx ne se faisant poinct comme de cire. » Pour moy, je saisis ledict fol et priay Dione de le mettre grommillant sur terre.

II. Late sixteenth century (in the manner of Montaigne):

Oyant dans la maistresse chambre un bruyt horrible qui là se faisoit et sembloit venir d'une beste sauvage laquelle vouloit s'eschapper, nous nous mismes en deliberation d'en prendre cognoissance deue et certaine de ce faict; et trouvasmes Eumolpe assis devant un grand parchemin, qui escriuoit des chronicques, lesquelles il mettoit quand et quand en vers. Nous aultres fusmes bien surprins de sa folie, pour ce qu'il pensoit qu'il luy estoit permis de rimailler ayant toutesfois a sa trace la furibonde et inexorable mort. Mais quoy ! le voyant ainsi testu, nous le saisismes et le poussames devant, luy, cependant braillant a pleine gorge, et luy conseillasmes de retourner à la raison. Mais ce fou desraisonnoit au poinct ou il crioit; « Laissez-moy asture que je finisse ces vers, car la fin n'en est pas aysee à parachever. » Quant est de moy, je saisis le fou et demandai à Dione de le poser grommelant sur terre.

REFERENCES

LIVET, C. L., *La grammaire française et les grammairiens du XVIe siècle* (Paris: Didier, 1859).

THUROT, CHARLES, *De la prononciation française depuis le commencement du XVIe siècle* (Imprimerie Nationale, Paris: 1881).

HUGUET, EDMOND, *Dictionnaire de la langue française du seizième siècle* (Paris: Champion, 1925–).

COTGRAVE, RANDLE, *A Dictionarie of the French and English Tongues* (London: Adam Islip, 1611; or a subsequent edition).

SARAUW, CHRISTINE, *Die Italianismen in der französischen Sprache des 16^t Jahrhundert* (Leipzig: R. Noske, 1920).

WIND, B. H., *Les mots italiens introduits en français au 16e S.* (Deventer: Kluwer, 1928).

In the *Mélanges* dedicated to F. Brunot (Paris, 1904) an article by Charles Beaulieux on dictionaries (pp. 371–398) and another by Mario Roques on grammarians (pp. 273–301). Consult also references given in our earlier chapters, where they continue to apply.

VII

THE SEVENTEENTH CENTURY

51. HISTORICAL SETTING

This century is perhaps the most important in the history of the French language. During that time there was impressed upon it that official stamp of academic regulation which has given it a character unique in Europe.

We have seen that evidences of a reaction against the enrichment tactics of the Renaissance were already visible in the sixteenth century, but the troubled history of the nation precluded any serious continuity in that direction or, for that matter, any extensive preoccupation with such matters. It was only with the advent of a more settled policy and social order that the forces of conservatism could operate.

For many years the court had followed the Valois kings around France. In 1600 it was permanently established at Paris, which thus became a more stable cultural focus, displacing in that capacity the valley of the Loire. Paris gathered increasingly the elite of the country and assumed more and more importance as a center of *beau langage*. The nucleus that formed around the monarch was comparatively small, but compact and homogeneous, a closely knit clannish body jealous of its social privileges. The result of this situation is something utterly strange to an American of the present day, the possibility of a single strong spirit being able to sway that small group and, through the centralized might of royalty, all that counted in the entire nation. Only in such a manner can we thoroughly account for the extraordinarily swift success of a man like Malherbe.

52 A. MALHERBE (1555-1628)

Malherbe was fifty years old when he came from his native Normandy to take a position at court. Of his disagreeable combative nature, his lack of lyric warmth, we need not speak here, since any history of literature will give the necessary information on his character. Suffice it to say that he soon developed an inordinate hatred for one Desportes, an " abbé de cour " of the infamous circle of Henri III, and proceeded to comment, in his manner, upon that gentleman's verses before a select group of his disciples, not in any organized way, but in detailed, scattered notes, such as are found in his marginalia on Desportes' works.   Here are a few specimens of his procedure:

> printanier: « Je n'aime point printanier. »
> clameur: « En latin bon, en français mauvais. »
> fère: « Se trouve assez en Ronsard, mais ni là ni ici il ne vaut rien. »
> alarme (un): « alarme est féminin. Qui en use autrement est un pauvre
>   homme. »
> poursuivir: « Mot normand. »   (He himself was a Norman.)
> Avéré: « Palais. »   (He himself was a man of legal family and legal
>   training.)

Even these few excerpts reveal that Malherbe turned his back on the archaisms, the coinages, and the dialectal borrowings of the *Deffence et Illustration*.   The scion of a legal family and a provincial, he repudiated any possible contribution of the legal language or of his native dialect.   Only the language of Paris and of a definite social group in Paris was acceptable.   The language of that group was sufficient even for literary use.

In the preceding century, the *noblesse de robe*, i.e., the parliamentary class, jurists and scholars as they were, had contributed immensely to the intellectual forces of the nation.[1]   Malherbe, a member of that stratum, turned his back upon the group he really represented and accepted the dictum of his court patrons, whom he chose to represent exclusively thenceforth.   The social prejudices of his new protectors were such that anything smacking of the tradesman was relegated to the " rear entrance," so to speak, of the language, the lower genres, burlesque, etc.   What we may say of the tradesman may be extended to include anything that savored of a trade jargon, of a technology.   In refined writing there was always present the risk that something uttered might not be grasped by the none too learned gentlemen that surrounded the king and their still less learned ladies, whose role was necessarily becoming more and more conspicuous.   Literature written for such minds could

---

[1] There was a time when they were considered as the group representing the best of the nation's language. Guillaume du Vair (1556–1621) had anticipated his friend Malherbe in his reform of prose. The latter was a "parlementaire," however, and not a "courtisan."

employ only a vehicle that was as socially admissible as the spoken language. Throughout the seventeenth century (and this should be noted with particular attention) the language of refined writing and refined speech does not differ in its essentials, despite the fact that its mechanics were never so carefully analyzed as in that period and despite the fact that never was its use so completely conscious and to a large extent so artificially controlled.

This petty noble, Malherbe, imbued as he was with the prejudices of his caste, went so far as to say that his masters in language were the porters of the grain docks on the Seine ("crocheteurs du Port au Foin"). The paradox is too evident to be taken literally. What is obviously to be understood is that all language, that of literature included, was to be made comprehensible even to the lowest strata of Parisian society. This was the answer to those who, in the middle of the last century, had dreamed of a learned style accessible to the cultivated alone.

Such policies tended to produce certain qualities which have remained ever since in the minds of French writers and teachers:

(1) *Clarity.* — "Je ne vous entends point" is Malherbe's favorite comment on Desportes. The Renaissance had wanted to make the language more "illustrious" by enrichment; "*pour Malherbe, au contraire, il faut illustrer la langue dans le sens étymologique du mot, en la rendant plus lumineuse.*" The fact that this quotation is from a *History of French Clarity*[2] is sufficiently significant.

(2) *Precision.* — As Mornet puts it (*loc. cit.*), "*fixer exactement à chaque élément de la langue son rôle et sa valeur dans la phrase.*" This end was obtained only by constant attention to the shadings of words, to vigilant discrimination between synonyms. To this labor, which Brunot (Vol. III, ch. VIII) refers to as a "*Travail Sémantique,*" Malherbe contributed not a little. Many a distinction previously unknown was made either by Malherbe or by those who followed his tradition. A few examples suffice:

Neuf and *nouveau*, often indistinguishable in the sixteenth century, acquired their present meanings. The same is true of *effroyable*, *terrible*, and *horrible*. The list is extensive.

Malherbe excluded any elements that might tend to produce any confusion in the mind of the reader or the hearer, whatever might be their value in "flavoring" or giving a special personal savor to a piece of prose or poetry. The archaic words so loved by the Pléiade for the atmosphere they were supposed to create had no

---

[2] Mornet, *Hist. de la clarté française*, p. 286.

value in his eyes because they were not universally understood. The seventeenth century was not in the main interested in historic local color. The present writer recalls a performance of Rameau's *Castor et Pollux* at the Paris *Opéra*, wherein the protagonists were dressed in the conventional Greek garb but the chorus appeared in the dress of Louis XIV's time and danced a *rigaudon!* " Atmosphere " being of little moment, comprehensibility was the real desideratum. Apropos of the old word *bénin*, Malherbe made the following significant comment: "*je serois d'avis de bannir ce mot de l'écriture, il l'est du langage.*" Thus literature had no right to use more extensive resources than those of the cultivated speaker; spoken and written French were identical.

What was the resultant product? A style without picturesqueness or even poetical charm, appealing primarily to the intelligence, serving as an expository medium, the clarity and elegance of which remain for subsequent centuries to admire.

It is strange that a detail worker such as we have just described should have left untouched something that cried for reform — the monumentally absurd spelling of the sixteenth century which, despite the efforts of a Meigret, had retained all its heavy pedantry. For a man of such destructive tendencies, for a *docteur en négative*, the failure even to mention the necessity of change seems an odd lapse. Possibly he felt that printing had sufficiently advanced to crystallize the external form of the word and that the public was becoming " eye-minded." Whatever the situation, from his day onward, attempts at simplification were sporadic and in general rather ineffective.

52 B. OPPOSITION

A man of Malherbe's type and tactics would necessarily arouse opposition. He did not win without a struggle. Mathurin Régnier (1573-1613), the nephew of Desportes, was an undisciplined soul, and his resentment against the " tyrant of syllables " served only to attract attention to his own carelessness. Mlle de Gournay (1566-1654), disciple and *fille d'alliance* of Montaigne represented the dead past, as did the Protestant poet D'Aubigné (1552-1630). One might dwell on the personal peculiarities that made the former a poor sort of apostle in the socially minded seventeenth century or the political conditions that excluded the latter, but the fact was that the drift was favorable to the hated *regratteur de syllabes* who

wished, as Mlle de Gournay said, to turn the language into a
" bouillon d'eau claire." Malherbe's muse may have been the
" *muse du raisonnement*,"[3] but it was acceptable as being also the
muse of Reason, the intellectual deity of the next two centuries.

53. CONTINUATORS

The attacks on Malherbe served to bring out the positive side of
his doctrine, which became the guide of a number of continuators,
each of whom developed it in his special way:

(1) J. Guez de Balzac (1594–1654), gentleman and *bel esprit*,
whose *Lettres* exemplify the vocabulary and syntactic principles of
the master. Balzac's contribution is in having adapted those dis-
tinctly French ideas to the Latin periodic sentence structure that
the Renaissance writers had cultivated. Balzac merely conserved
the main elements of its effectiveness, its rolling rhythm and ma-
jestic sonority, the subordination of its several elements. Balzac
achieved his end without falling into the old excesses of ponderosity
and obscurity that had characterized the " Ciceronians " of the
preceding age; he did so by reducing the ample scale of the Latin
period to smaller, more French proportions. His immense popularity shows to what extent his taste was in accord with the trend
of his time. A letter of Balzac was the best present a lover could
offer his lady. The *beaux esprits* were apparently capable of appre-
ciating his style and of seeing the difference between it and that of
the numerous *Secrétaires* that showed the contemporary gallant
how to indite an epistle in the approved manner of the *Astrée*. It
appealed also to the refined swains of the court or the subsidiaries
thereof to use that style at once elegant and simple to the point of
poverty. With Balzac, the French language begins to become a
gueuse fière, a beggar in its lack of richness, but proud of its social
graces.

The new tendencies find scholarly expression in the work of Antoine Oudin, polyglot " *interprète de Sa Majesté pour les langues
allemande, italienne et espagnolle.*" The title *Grammaire française
rapportée au langage du temps* (1632) is significant in that a feature
of the work is its modernity. Thus the way is prepared for Vaugelas
and his policies. Oudin has the same flair as his successor for the
construction that is to become correct in our own time: *C'est à moi*
is preferred to *c'est mien;* the conditional in the result of an *if*

---

[3] Brunot, *Commentaire*, p. 157 ff.

clause acquires even a certain preference over the heavy imperfect subjunctive.

If the written language was thus being pruned and "purified," similar influences were concentrating on the spoken language. The problem was not the same in both cases, at least not entirely. Literary style, as we have seen, needed to be rid of personal mannerisms and scholastic impedimenta; the spoken tongue needed to be purged of improprieties. The higher strata of society were scarcely uniformly elegant in the days of Henry IV and the earlier part of the reign of Louis XIII. Immediately following the civil wars, many an old fighter suddenly found himself a courtier altogether too suddenly to lose the picturesque language of the camp. Mme de Rambouillet, a lady of Italian origin brought up in refined surroundings, found the environment of the royal court too crude for her sensibilities and withdrew in disgust to found a circle of her own. This became the most important speech refining laboratory of the period.

54. THE SALON OF MME DE RAMBOUILLET

In the *chambre bleue* of Arthénice, as she was called, social discipline was the keynote. Vossler [4] goes so far as to say that preciosity, the superrefinement which reigned in that famous house, was not merely a European phenomenon but more especially the human ideal of the Counterreformation, in that discipline and Reason were its ideals. Under such circumstances the ridiculous side of the movement, as we see it in Molière or Somaize, is far from the important aspect of preciosity. From the linguistic point of view, it is a phase of the same ideas that dominated Malherbe, a fact less curious since the commentator of Desportes was a frequent guest of Mme de Rambouillet's salon. Hence the same social ban on display of learning (*secouer la poussière des bibliothèques*) and on impropriety. As to the latter, the scruples of the sensitive women were frequently exaggerated; one "suffered furiously" at a word even vaguely offering a possible suggestion of the indecent and a poor fellow could not speak with impunity of "*poitrine de veau*" or assert that he "loved" melon. In the latter case, he would have to say "*J'estime le melon.*" It is, of course, true that propriety, as practiced in the seventeenth century, however it might be a reaction against the license of the sixteenth, was not what our present standards would

[4] *Frankreichs Kultur*, p. 321.

lead us to expect: certain sallies of Voiture, one of the salon's *habitués*, are hardly meant for very refined company, though it may have been that this commoner was allowed certain liberties.

It is undoubtedly true that, where the unadorned word might be frowned upon, where it was suggestive of the improper, periphrases and euphonious circumlocutions were currently used and the process of periphrasing extended to cases not necessarily reprehensible. Yet to say that a chair was regularly referred to as a " *commodité de la conversation* " or a mirror called " *le conseiller des graces,*" as one might gather from the *Précieuses Ridicules* or Somaize's *Dictionnaire des Pretieuses,* is surely an exaggeration; it is easy to take a metaphor out of its context and make it look absurd. Most likely these locutions are of the type found in pastoral novels like the famous *Astrée,* reflecting the prevailing literary styles, Gongorism, Marinism, etc., and representing different species of hyperelegant inflated manners of expression.

Précieux society was not merely concerned with vocabulary. The Danish grammarian, Nyrop,[5] relates how a certain guest in the Hôtel de Rambouillet, hesitating whether to say *aveine* or *avoine,* exclaimed in disgust: " *Avoine, avoine, de par tous les diables! on ne sçait comment parler céans.*" Let us note that, as between the etymological form (from *avēna*) which should have given *aveine,* and *avoine,* not explainable according to Francian phonology, it was the latter that was chosen. Literary circles sought all possible authority on pronunciation and even the mechanics of it. In the *Bourgeois gentilhomme,* Molière puts on the stage a real textbook on phonetics, the *Discours physique de la parole* of Geraut de Cordemoy, which appears in the famous lesson scene where poor Jourdain is being initiated into the mysteries of vowels and consonants. It is quite probable that some of the audience recognized the book, which may perhaps have been one of the texts known to the learned ladies. Spelling reform was a question that absorbed the attention of the women, who were unconcerned with the retention of evidence as to any etymology, real or fancied. As the salons were influential, certain reforms found official recognition. This is the *orthographe des dames* alluded to below.

From our present specialized outlook, preciosity may be summed up as follows: From the literary stylistic angle it represented a phase of the European wave of inflated, unnatural rhetoric which in England was called Euphuism, in Spain, Gongorism, and in Italy,

[5] *Gr. hist.,* I, § 55.

Marinism. In France, it had a more serious and more far-reaching effect. The best proof is that we find in the salons, especially that of Mme de Rambouillet, a large nucleus of men who were to form the Académie Française, carrying over into that body many attitudes and processes that we may still distinguish there.

55. THE " ACADÉMIE FRANÇAISE "

In 1635 a group of men who had met habitually since 1629 at the house of the highly cultured bourgeois Valentin Conrart were asked by Cardinal Richelieu to form an official academy after the pattern of the Italian academies of the Renaissance. The Cardinal's purposes were to create something very serious, a piece of governmental machinery to legislate for language as other bodies legislated on matters economic or judicial. Conrart's group, itself a typical Renaissance " men's club," understood but too well the purposes of His Eminence and had small inclination to lose its freedom, but it was obliged to yield. However, modeling their organization upon traditional Italian assemblies which were called by such names as Intronati (the Thunderstruck, the " dizzy " as it were) or the Humoristici, the academicians could not lose the playful side of things which had always entered into the doings of their illustrious predecessors as far back as Plato. Like their prototypes, they mixed the social and the scientific. Such a body could not represent a university tradition nor even a purely scholarly point of view for its own sake; rather it represented the attitude of the cultivated gentleman. The professor or lawyer got as much consideration here as from Malherbe or at the Hôtel de Rambouillet. Thus we have the spectacle of the official linguistic organization of a large centralized state standing for an extrascholastic social tradition. This situation is without parallel in Europe.

The program of the Académie Française, as outlined in its Statutes, is ambitious: There were to be composed a dictionary, a grammar, a rhetoric and a manual of poetic theory. At the same time, the works of prominent writers were to be examined and reported on, an activity which is outside of our province, except in so far as the language of the author criticized might come in for discussion.

56. THE ACADEMY DICTIONARY

In 1638, the work on the dictionary was begun under the leadership of Claude Favre, Baron de Vaugelas, of whom much will be said later. From the admirable account of two academicians, Pellisson and D'Olivet, we gather that there was little practical organization of the task and hardly any efficiency. The result was an exasperating slowness which invited numerous lampoons. One wag suggested that, the dictionary being then at the letter *F*, he would be delighted to live until they reached *G*. There was one time when Vaugelas' papers were seized by creditors and the work was practically paralyzed. Finally, in 1694, that is to say fifty-eight years after its inception, the book was off the press and was presented to the king with ceremony.[6] As was to be expected, it was ultra-conservative and based essentially on the canons of Malherbe, with even more restrictions on the admission of popular terms. A few spelling reforms under salon pressure were incorporated, a concession to the much-advocated " *orthographe des dames.*" The " *lettres ramistes* " (cf. preceding chapter on Ramus) were adopted (*i, j; u, v*). What made the first edition hard to use was the arrangement of words in " families " under their " roots," so that a word like *bienséant* was to be located under *seoir, insensiblement* under *sens*.[7] A sort of index was appended, but it was so crudely done that it served little purpose. The second edition adopted the alphabetical order.

57. THE ACADEMY GRAMMAR

The grammar, which alone of the three other projects concerns us here, was published under the Academy sanction in 1932. It was received with much adverse criticism, having the misfortune to be published in an era when linguistics is a scientific pursuit. It was precisely a scientific scholar, M. Brunot, who, with his *Observations*, set loose a flood of criticism which the Academy has not, at present writing, answered.

58. VAUGELAS

This should not be taken to mean that the 1932 grammar was the first to be undertaken by the Academy. Several were attempted

[6] A facsimile edition was produced by Paul Dupont in 1901, in 2 vols.

[7] The method was used again by Raynouard, in the early nineteenth century, for his Provençal lexicon, despite the obvious inconvenience.

with academic sanction, but always on the responsibility of individuals. In the seventeenth century, it was Vaugelas who took it upon himself to record contemporary usage. That gentleman was a native of the duchy of Savoy, therefore not even a Frenchman, much less a Parisian. Yet as soon as he reached the capital, he began, like Malherbe, to out-Herod Herod and pose as the champion of Parisian French and even more than that, to delimit the court speech from that of *la ville*, which constituted the upper middle class and was more or less an adjunct of the court. The already limited category that he selected as his standard for good usage was further reduced by his adoption of the standard " *la plus saine partie de la cour,*" as he expressed it, tempering that phrase with the addition " *conformément à la façon d'escrire de la plus saine partie des Autheurs de ce temps.*" Such was the reply to the plea for a democratic attitude in language that had been made by a free spirit, La Mothe le Vayer, who had bewailed the narrow point of view which he saw the purists taking. How completely La Mothe's protests went unheeded is shown by Vaugelas' declaration of policy:

(1) " *Que le peuple n'est point le maistre de la langue* " (Ch. VIII, Introd.).

(2) There will always remain a stable court element to keep usage from running wild.

(3) A new word can enter the language under favorable conditions, that is if it is launched by a noble of sufficiently high rank or by the sovereign himself.

(4) The individual does not, except under such conditions as mentioned in (3), dare to protest. " *Il ne faut pas s'attacher à son sentiment particulier contre l'usage.*"

On the other hand, if Vaugelas is undemocratic, he is not, grammatically speaking, dogmatic. The title of his work *Remarques* (1647) precludes a preconceived consecutively arranged system. We are dealing with no systematic codification. The presentation of Vaugelas is in the form of disconnected observations; Malherbe's commentary on Desportes was similarly allowed to remain until recent times in the form of marginal notes, as we have indicated. So it is with this whole generation of *Remarques, Observations, Doutes, Sentiments, Entretiens,* and *Réflexions* — all, including the Academy's own *Décisions,* scattered and disjointed, lacking nothing so much as good indices.[8] It seems as if contemporaries did not

---

[8] We offer a classified index of the *Remarques* in the appendix.

feel as yet the need of guiding principles or of generalizations. The following conclusions may be gleaned from Vaugelas:

(1) That some power exists in language superior to the will of the individual, perhaps even to that of the artist. Language is social.

(2) The whim of the critic is of no decisive value. (Here he is not in tune with Malherbe.) Careful observation alone, without dogmatism, can be accepted.

(3) The subjects of observation must be of the ruling class and their usage alone is worthy of record.

(4) The present alone is of importance. Vaugelas had an uncanny flair for the future; that is, for the usage that was to survive. As for the past, what those of former days thought and felt was of no moment.

The authority of the *Remarques* was immense. Writers of note corrected their works to conform to its judgments. Racine had a volume with him at Uzès to counteract the influence of the southern dialects with which he was surrounded. The very jests about Vaugelas bear witness to his popularity: In Molière's *Femmes savantes* (Act II, sc. vi), the servant Martine is reproached as follows:

> Elle a, d'une insolence à nulle autre pareille,
> Après trente leçons, insulté mon oreille
> Par l'impropriété d'un mot sauvage et bas,
> Qu'en termes décisifs condamne Vaugelas.

and Balzac hoped (cf. note to this passage in the Grands Ecrivains edition) that the word *féliciter* (to congratulate) would soon be acceptable since Vaugelas had promised not to oppose it.

59. BOUHOURS

This influential grammarian was ably supplemented by a Jesuit, Père Bouhours, like his predecessor one to whom the French language was a *grande passion*, and who took as great pleasure in picking holes in the Jansenist literary style as in Jansenist theology. To him Racine sent his *Phèdre* for correction with this observation:

> Je vous envoie les quatre premiers actes de ma tragédie et je vous envoierai le cinquième dès que je l'aurai transcrit. Je vous supplie, mon R. P., de prendre la peine de les lire et de marquer les fautes que je puis avoir faites contre la langue dont vous êtes un de nos plus excellents maîtres ... (Rosset, p. 6).

Bouhours was concerned with literary style rather than with

conversational usage. He is not always as fragmentary as Vaugelas. If he did write a series of *Doutes sur la langue française proposés à Messieurs de l'Académie* (Paris, 1674) and two series of *Remarques* (Paris, 1676 and Amsterdam, 1693), he is also the author of a connected treatise, the second of the *Entretiens d'Ariste et d'Eugène*, dealing with language. Here Bouhours feels called upon to reply to the charge that French vocabulary is poor by saying: " *On ne demeure jamais court, on exprime tout ce qu'on veut en notre langue quand on la sait bien* " (Rosset, p. 41). He saw only good in the rejection of old and improper words and was in these respects the perfect purist. Indeed, as to his materials he contributed almost nothing new to the general policy of the purist predecessors, though in his procedure and objectives he is in harmony with the *raisonneurs* (see below).

The century saw a flood of grammarians each with his *Observations, Nouvelles observations, Sentimens*, and *Nouveaux sentimens*. Previous discussions were rediscussed and new comments added. If there were a few notables like Thomas Corneille (brother of the dramatist who wrote the *Cid*) or Oliver Patru (1604–1681), we have among the members of the grammatical group a host of nonentities.

60. THE DISSIDENTS

There were a few who opposed either the letter or the spirit of Vaugelas and his fellow purists. La Mothe le Vayer (1587–1672) took the stand, in opposition to Vaugelas, that the courtier was a person of superficial culture, without discipline in the scholarly sense; in other words, one likely to regard consistency as one of the minor virtues and to change his mind from time to time with reference to a linguistic phenomenon. Both La Mothe and Ménage (1613–1692) protested in various ways against the mere presentation of findings without correlation or interpretation, saying that it is impossible to glean anything from an observation unless its import is brought out by the observer. Ménage, a man of vast erudition and one of the few who, in that day, had first-hand knowledge of Old French and the early stages of other Romance languages, attempted to show how Vaugelas fell short in not bringing in the perspective offered by an examination of a fact in the light of its history [9]: His statement is interestingly worded: " *On est toujours*

[9] Ménage himself had desired to do so in his *Origines de la langue françoise* 1650. The improved edition of 1694 is called *Dictionnaire étymologique ou Origines* . . . It is still useful to scholars.

enfant dans sa langue . . . quand on ne lit que les Auteurs de son tems, et que l'on ne parle que la langue de sa nourrice. On donne un tour plus net et plus sublime à son discours quand on sait la généalogie des termes dont on se sert . . ." But, despite a certain material success, he made no lasting impression on his period, unless one considers it a lasting impression to be ridiculed by Molière, who in *Les Femmes savantes* portrayed him as the ridiculous pedant Vadius. Etymology, which Ménage liked immensely and in which he did some exceedingly keen if not always scientific work, was at that time considered the recreation of a not too well-balanced mind. It should be said, in justice to the seventeenth century, that Ménage had scarcely the apostolic temperament sufficient to combat the prejudices of his environment despite his ability as a fighter. In fact, as Brunot remarks, this author of a commentary on Rabelais was nevertheless himself a purist, and the objectives of purism, even to its concomitant preciosity, were not inimical to him.[10] So it was that he did not alter the trend, and the rest of the century was consumed in the old tiresome round.

The sentimental Fénelon must have jarred considerably certain of his contemporaries. He did not believe, with Vaugelas, that there was any fixity to a language. The very dictionary of the Academy would one day be nothing more than an antiquarian's aid in deciphering texts of its period; the grammar could not fix a living tongue, though it might halt capricious changes "*par lesquels la mode règne sur les termes comme sur les habits.*" Answering the observations of Malherbe and Vaugelas, he asserted that the old language, for him that of Amyot and Marot, "*se fait regretter,*" that not only has a wrong been done to the language in allowing its impoverishment, but that such a wrong ought to be righted by a judicious process of enrichment.

To the credit of the linguistic doctrinaires whom we have discussed, it should be said that they did not merely preach, but with commendable zeal put their prescriptions into practice by offering what they believed to be the nearest thing to perfect exemplars — the product of long untiring labor. One contribution took thirty years! We note, with some astonishment, that these models of the perfect style were not original writings but translations from the ancients, as, for example, the rendition of Quintus Curtius's *History of Alexander the Great*, which we owe to Vaugelas. Considering this era of historical insensitiveness and considering the objectives of

[10] *Hist.* IV, 5.

these Latin versions one may suspect with considerable plausibility that the desire to portray a Quintus Curtius faithfully was not of primary importance. These specimens of *beau langage* were to be more elegant than the productions of the classics: " . . . *l'éducation des anciens était à faire. On devait leur apprendre un peu de ce fin du fin, de cette politesse, de cette délicatesse que ces gentilhommes* (i.e., the ancients) *auraient connu sans doute, s'ils avaient eu le bonheur de naître au XVIIe siècle.*" [10]

61. DICTIONARIES

A few dictionaries give a glimpse into a vocabulary more meaty and vigorous than the somewhat anemic, if refined, residuum of the purists. Furetière, author of the *Roman Bourgeois* and himself of bourgeois sympathies, was a member of the Academy for many years. He soon tired of the lack of teamwork and the narrow social viewpoint. He was already working on his own when his confreres heard of it and expelled him in 1685. Undeterred, Furetière engaged in a furious battle with his old comrades and continued his labors, ending up in Holland (because of the academic monopoly in France), where he died in 1688. His dictionary was published in Amsterdam in 1690. The difference between it and the work of the Academy is evident: technical and trade terms find greater representation and even a few bourgeois words and *mots bas*, as was to be expected from *le moins poli de tous les hommes*. During his numerous quarrels with his old colleagues, Furetière had contended that his was a *Dictionnaire Universel* and not one of refined usage and therefore not intended to compete with that of the Academy. The latter refused to admit so fine a distinction.

Both dictionaries had been anticipated by Richelet (1680). Brunot and Bruneau [11] speak of Richelet's as " *le premier Diction-naire qui ne soit pas accompagné d'une traduction en une autre langue,*" a veritable encyclopedia, not merely liberal in its general lexicon but in the use of proper nouns such as one would find in the La-rousse of today. A point worthy of special mention is the gathering of examples, in modern fashion, from reputable authors, rather than from the lexicographer's fancy, backing up those illustrations, as did the Academy, by the prestige of the body as a whole. There is one great difference from the modern dictionary: it is not objec-

---

[10a] Hennebert, *Hist. des traductions françaises, cit.* Minckwitz, *Beitr. z. Gesch. der franz. Grammatik, ZfrS,* XIX, 89.

[11] *Gr. hist.* Introduction, p. xxii.

tive but is filled with biting satire against persons or social groups, such as provincials, clerics. Brunot speaks of the term *Prédicateur*. On looking it up in the edition of 1709, the present writer finds this definition: " *C'est un ecclésiastique qui est, ou qui doit etre, un homme de probité.*" Apropos of *chèvre* the following quip appears:

> Si pour avoir le nom d'un sage,
> Il suffit de porter une barbe au menton,
> Une chèvre sur nous auroit grand avantage,
> Elle vaudroit plus que Platon.

wherein we are reminded of the tone of Cotgrave, except that Richelet is more biting, more ironic.

62. "GRAMMAIRE RAISONNÉE"

At one time in the century there came a reaction against the method of disconnected grammatical comment which we have described. The demand was for general results from all this labor and for an interpretation of such results. Had Ménage comprehended his role and been able to impose his view on his contemporaries, the historical method would have satisfied that demand by interpreting the present in the light of the past, establishing in this manner a chronological system that would constitute a kind of unity. We have seen, however, from the anecdote of *Castor et Pollux* (see p. 82) how little interest there was in historical development. Just as the monarchy of the Sun King was thought superior to any government of the past, and the governments of the past represented merely embryonic stages of the fully matured kingship of Louis XIV, so the language of the time was considered as having reached its zenith and the past represented merely the struggles to reach that perfection. Kingdom and language were permanent and fixed; history is interesting only for one who thinks of things as in a state of flux. For a situation of fixity, description was the only possible procedure, with logic as the instrument of ultimate interpretation. Let us stress the fact that the universities were still in the throes of dialectics, and syllogisms were still shuttled across the classrooms of the day; the intellectuals held Reason as Allah and Descartes as the Mohammed of their cult. It is no trouble to conceive how naturally the Cartesian could figure that language was a product of the mind and of Reason, wherefor it could be, like Reason, not merely analyzed but even guided and controlled. When the Cartesian is at the same time a pedagogue, as were the Jansenists of Port-Royal, we can see how he would seek to present a language clearly and eagerly accept a means of demonstrating that its mechanics were founded on a perfect system.

It is not enough, said the Port-Royalists, to learn the mechanics of good speech ... "*ne pas en avoir seulement l'usage, mais d'en pénétrer aussi les raisons et de faire par science ce que les autres font seulement par coutume.*" The "science" displayed in the famous *Grammaire de Port-Royal* (1660) of Nicole and Arnaud is clearly to be appraised from the following passage from the Introduction: "*Les progrès et la décadence d'une langue sont inséparables des progrès et de la décadence du goût. Pour s'assurer de l'état d'une langue, il faut examiner si, depuis sa* fixation *l'on n'a point altéré son génie, en inventant de nouveaux mots, en déformant l'acception des termes admis, en confondant les* genres *de style.*" [12] Of the word *fixation* we have spoken sufficiently. What interests us more is the idea of a norm inherent in a language, a norm which is invariable for each *genre* and inviolate, depending on *taste* — presumably that of the courtiers. Here as elsewhere there seems to be no separate criterion for the spoken language; it seems to be understood that the literary style is all that counts.

The *raisonneur* idea in language was not carried to extremes by the teachers of Port-Royal in their *Petites Écoles*. They were of the few pedagogues who included French in their curriculum, and, treating it as a living tongue, they did not allow preconceived theories to distort the fact that fixity was a difficult affair to postulate.

63. POPULAR SPEECH

In this chapter, we have thus far lost sight of the fact that the actual number of people with whom we have been concerned was but a small part of even the Parisian population. When we read Molière, a linguistic realist in the main, we see the numerous social strata — the upper and the lower bourgeoisie, the servant, the peasant from the outskirts of Paris. M. Jourdain, immortal hero of the *Bourgeois gentilhomme*, can be distinguished by his love of the archaic expression, the proverb, the " rubber stamp " of middle-class civility ("*J'aime mieux être incivil qu'importun* "). During the Fronde, we have the satires against Cardinal Mazarin — *Mazarinades*,

---

[12] The emphasis on *fixation* and *genres* is the authors'.

as they are known — in which there are specimens of a crude dialect, that of the Place Maubert fishwives, the Parisian Billingsgate. Unfortunately our data with reference to this speech can hardly be reliable, the " brogue " being exaggerated for comic effect. It is interesting to observe that this dialect from the outskirts of the capital forms the base of by far the largest part of peasant speech as shown in the comic theater of the time. (Needless to say, dialect was always comic, and was never presented with an eye to real local color.) Even in the lower genres, we see, the rest of France virtually does not exist, except for the rare specimen of Languedoc *patois* used by Molière in his comedy *Monsieur de Pourceaugnac* and meant, it would seem, for " slapstick " scenes, somewhat like the gibberish that occurs in the *Farce of Pathelin*, when the hero pretends to be raving with fever.

64. FRENCH ABROAD

The language of Paris, purified and, to be sure, rarefied in the manner indicated, became, in the seventeenth century, the envy of all Europe, a bright jewel in the crown of the Roi-Soleil. Along with that monarch's court manners, his language began to penetrate into the courts of kings and princelings. The nobles of the Rhineland aped Versailles and their ladies played pastoral dramas in French. The Restoration of Charles II returned to London a family brought up in contact with French royalty. Louis XIV encouraged colonization and the development of the merchant marine, so that the language spread to far-off shores. French Protestants had already found their home country inhospitable to them and had been emigrating. The revocation of the Edict of Nantes (1685) merely hastened an already existing state of affairs. The exodus assumed great proportions, people going to England, Holland, Germany and, in North America, principally to Virginia and North and South Carolina.

65. ALSACE

Alsace had been acquired in 1648, but the monarchy allowed a surprising amount of provincial seclusion, so that French made rather small progress.

66. FOREIGN INFLUENCE ON FRENCH

As to the influence of foreign tongues upon French, that of Spanish is the only one to be reckoned with seriously.[13]   One is disposed, in view of the literary situation, to exaggerate Spain's linguistic effect. It is true that the one could not be powerful without affecting the other.   The language was *à la mode*.   Conversation books had a large sale.   Oudin, whom we have encountered before, wrote a *Trésor des deux langues*, that is to say, a Franco-Spanish lexicon. The queens of Louis XIII and XIV were Spanish in language and a host of court satellites filled the entourage of those monarchs, recalling a situation such as we found in the reign of Francis I with regard to Italian.   Among the Spanish words entering French are: *bizarre* and *fanfaron* (indicative of attitudes regarded as Spanish), *anchois* and *artichaut* (indicative of commercial relations).[14]

67 A. LINGUISTIC RESULTS

This century was one of decisions.   Not that these decisions were based on any greater intuition or knowledge or any greater insight.   The temper of the times called for the clearing up of confusion, whether the results were based on anything or on nothing. The process proved efficacious even if arbitrary and was moreover carried out by people with an extraordinary flair for that which was to survive into the present.   A few specimens, among the many that could be adduced, are here given:

(1) *Pronunciation and Vocabulary* — We remember the rime in Villon's *Lais* (178–180): *barre; ferre*.   That hesitation was still current in the seventeenth century.   In the case of *sarge* vs. *serge*, it was definitely decided in favor of the latter.   So also the quarrels of the *o-istes* and the *ouistes*, who had filled the preceding century and no small part of this one with their controversy as to whether one should spell *chose* or *chouse, arroser* or *arrouser, soris* or *souris*, were all "settled," some in favor of *o* some of *ou*, without one's being able to tell on what basis for a large part of the words.   Nasalization is completed, with *in* becoming definitely *ē*.

During this century the pronunciation [ɛ] for *oi* came to be preferred, in most instances, to [wɛ]; this was especially true in the case of the imperfect and conditional endings, as in *je disois, tu*

---

[13] Richard Ruppert, *Die spanischen Lehn- und Fremdwörter in der frz. Schriftsprache* (diss., Munich, 1915).

[14] For a fairly long list, see the *Dictionnaire général*, p. 25.

disois, etc. A very important development was the "*r grasseyé*," or uvular *r*, which began to be used in the upper strata of Parisian society in the third quarter of the seventeenth century. Our evidence for this dating is a play of that period in which an affected speaker's *gr*'s are represented by a *gue*. At first this pronunciation must have been the subject of much ridicule, but it ended by spreading widely and was even adopted in Germany in the early eighteenth century.[15] Consonants at the end of a word were now silent before a pause as well as before another word beginning with a consonant; their usual pronunciation before a following vowel we call liaison. Final *r* and *l* shared this same fate: *fini*(*r*), *coupe*(*r*), *porteu*(*r*), *i*(*l*), *péri*(*l*), *saou*(*l*), but in the eighteenth century these two consonants were restored in a number of instances. The palatal *l*, in such words as *fille* and *merveille*, gave way in the seventeenth century to a simple yod or *y* sound among the middle classes. Thus the bourgeoisie tended to say [fiịə] and [filịə], but this alteration was not fully accepted by the upper class until the nineteenth century.

The grammarians succeeded in forcing from the language many expressions such as *cheoir* (to fall), *combien que* (although), *au demeurant* (for the rest), *marri* (bewildered), *ressentiment* (gratitude), etc.; but in spite of their conservative efforts additional neologisms came into the language to stay. J. Guez de Balzac introduced *anachronisme;* Molière used *choquant;* Charles Sorel introduced *cuistre.* To give even a partial list of such new words would be too detailed for the purposes of this book. Suffice it to say that Balzac, Molière, Sorel, Pascal, André Félibien, Ménage, Voiture, Furetière, P. Corneille, and Bossuet were among those who contributed the most to this new vocabulary. The grammarians fixed the meanings of many words which had been used rather broadly in the previous era, such as *équipage, fondre, juste, politesse, rupture.* They distinguished carefully between *attache* and *attachement, avis* and *advertissement, barbare* and *sauvage, coutume* and *observation*, and many other partial synonyms.

(2) *Syntax.* — Syntax is the seventeenth century's greatest contribution outside of, perhaps, the elements of semantic delimitation. *Depuis Vaugelas* is a recurrent phrase in the historical grammars. It is probable that our freshmen will not thank the gentleman al-

---

[15] H. C. Lancaster in *MLN*, XLIX, 243–8. Some historians of the French language refuse to believe that the uvular *r* developed in France before the eighteenth century and they assert that it was a middle-class phenomenon. See Dauzat, *op. cit.*, § 122.

luded to for so clearly, if arbitrarily, regulating the behavior of a past participle in compound tenses. Marot had already expressed himself on the subject (cf. § 41), but his dictum had remained without effect and had even encountered hostility. Furthermore, he had said nothing about a following object. Vaugelas takes all the manifestations of the past participle *par ordre* in accordance with the spirit of the age. Those same elementary students would be interested to know that Vaugelas legislated with authority on the order of personal pronouns. In Old French the situation had been clear: the direct object preceding when there were two personal pronouns before the verb. By the Renaissance the situation had become altogether chaotic. The decision of the *Remarques* was as follows: " *Il faut dire:* je vous le promets *et non pas* ie le vous promets, *comme disent tous les anciens Escrivains et plusieurs modernes encore.*" [16] Similarly the distinction between *qui* and *quoi* is made clear and the statement made that the phrase *à qui* must have a personal antecedent. *Aucun* becomes negative in value, competing with *nul*. One could go on for a long time this way, enumerating the fixing of many points that are now taken for granted in our modern French syntax. The discussion fills a whole volume of Brunot's *Histoire de la langue française* (IV, part 2).

There are several such constructions which deserve to receive special stress, illustrating as they do not only the temper of the time but also the manner in which certain of our modern scholars are perceiving the relationship between the psychology of a given period and the resultant linguistic phenomena: M. Lucien Foulet has published in *Romania*, LXVI (1920), 46 ff., a study on the passing of the construction *ce suis-je* to *c'est moi*, in which he believes the interesting point to lie in the increasing emphasis on the person, letting the action, as represented by the verb, pass into the background and become impersonal. One may take such an evolution, which was completed in the seventeenth century, as showing the trend, characteristic of the Renaissance, toward stressing the personality. Perhaps we may include here on the same basis the strict determination of the exact province of *qui* and *quoi*, which we have mentioned and the equally strict delineation of reflexive and purely active verbs, excluding such pseudo reflexives as *se dormir* and *se marcher* (meaning no more than *dormir* and *marcher*) on the ground that they do not show the activity of the agent with sufficient

---

[16] Ed. Chassang, 96.

force.[17] The modern subjunctive rules were clarified, believes Voss-ler,[18] under the influence of Descartes's analysis of the emotions.

Probably a more important creation than any of those we have mentioned (and, unlike so many seventeenth-century phenomena in linguistics, it is a positive creation) is the building of the sentence. From the tortuous style of Descartes to the organ-like magnificence of Bossuet's *Oraison funèbre*, the evolution is considerable. In the earlier part of the century, it had been a " *phrase lentement déroulée, solidement étayée, la phrase d'une pensée qui travaille à se mettre en ordre et prétend, avant tout, manifester son enchaînement.*" It is, remarks Lanson, a " *carapace logique.*" [19] We have spoken of J. Guez de Balzac and what he did for the periodic structure. The stylists worked to attain fullness of rhythm, at the same time re-ducing the mechanical contrivances, the relative pronouns, and the conjunctions that had up to that time cluttered up the machinery of expression.

Thus we approach the eighteenth century with a vocabulary quantitatively impoverished, but worked over in such a way as to make it very effective in the limited sphere of analysis and of elo-quence. The sentence is now a fitting mold for those special prov-inces.

67 B. TRANSLATION: SEVENTEENTH CENTURY

Ayant entendu, dans la grand'salle, un vacarme inoui qui sembloit venir d'une bête fauve qui en désiroit échapper, nous mîmes tous nos soins à enquérir la cause de cela. L'on trouva Eumolpe, à part soi, rem-plissant de je ne sais quels méchants vers un fort grand parchemin. Nous autres, demeurant dans l'admiration de voir ainsi quelqu'un qui n'avoit garde de laisser là ses rimes, voire devant le danger de mort, le poussâmes avant, quoiqu'il se démenoit comme un enragé, et l'engageâmes à se con-duire en honnête homme. Mais considérez, je vous prie, la folie de ce rimailleur qui crioit: « Laissez, laissez! J'eusse voulu finir ces vers, car enfin, foi de gentilhomme, ils clochent quelque peu vers la fin. » Pour ma part, je m'emparai de ce plaisant et je demandai à Dione de le déposer, (il est vrai que ce n'étoit qu'avec force imprécations) grommelant sur terre.

[17] Vossler, p. 268.
[18] *Ibid.*, p. 286.
[19] *Art de la prose*, p. 55.

REFERENCES

BRUNOT, F., *La doctrine de Malherbe d'après son commentaire sur Desportes* (Paris: G. Masson, 1891).

BRUNOT, F., *Histoire de la langue française des origines à 1900.* Tomes III & IV (Paris: A. Colin, *1905*).

CAYROU, G., *Le français classique* (Paris: H. Didier, 1924).

Dictionnaire de l'Académie Française (7th ed. Paris, 1878; 8th ed., Paris, 1931–38; 1st ed., in facsimile, Paris, 1901.)

FÉNELON, *Lettre à M. Dacier sur les occupations de l'Académie* in *Œuvres* (Paris: Didot, 1861), III, 210 ff.

HAASE, A., *Französische Syntax des 17ten Jahrhunderts* (Oppeln & Leipzig: E. Franck, 1888). Fr. trans. rev. by M. Obert (Paris: Delagrave, 1916).

HARNOIS, G., *Les théories du langage en France de 1660 à 1821* (Paris: Soc. d'éd. " Les Belles Lettres," 1938).

MORNET, D., *Histoire de la clarté française* (Paris: Payot, 1929).

NYROP, KR., *Grammaire historique de la langue française* (2nd éd. rev. et augm.; Copenhague: Gyldendalske boghandel, Nordisk forlag, 1904–30. New York: G. E. Stechert, 1904. Paris: Picard et fils, 1904).

PELLISSON, P. and ABBÉ D'OLIVET, *Histoire de l'Académie Française* (Paris: Didier, 1858).

ROSSET, T., *Les origines de la prononciation moderne étudiées au 17ᵉ siècle* (Paris: A. Colin, 1911).

ROSSET, T., *Entretiens, Doutes, Critiques et Remarques du Père Bouhours sur la langue française, 1671–1692* (Grenoble: Allier frères, 1908).

RUPPERT, R., *Die spanischen Lehn- u. Fremdwörter in der frz. Schriftsprache* (diss. Munich, 1915).

SAMFIRESCO, E., *Ménage, polémiste, philologue, poète* (Paris: Fontemoing, 1903).

SCHMIDT, W. F., " *Die spanische Elemente im franz. Wortschatz,*" in: *Zeitschr. f. rom. Phil.* (1914).

VAUGELAS, C. F. DE, *Remarques sur la langue française,* ed. Chassang (Paris: J. Baudry, 1880). Facsimile of orig. ed., Société des textes français modernes (Paris: Droz, 1934).

VIII

THE EIGHTEENTH CENTURY

68. HISTORY

In 1715 the great career of the Roi-Soleil reached its end in a gloomy anticlimax. Louis XIV's son and grandson having died before him, the great-grandson, a boy of five, ascended the throne. A regency was established under Phillip of Orléans, who proceeded to set an example of debauchery that was followed with zeal by the king throughout his life. The tone of the court degenerated with the absence of the discipline which the old monarch had upheld, and with this relaxation went a good deal of the genuine refinement that had characterized the preceding reign. Indeed there came a time during the eighteenth century when a young Dauphin excelled in his repertory of mouth-filling oaths.

The royalty, with such a mode of life, showed little concern for the public treasury. Taxes were increased to make up for royal extravagance. The king connived at shady dealings with corporate bodies fostering business schemes analogous to that of John Law. When ruin was imminent, clever economists like Turgot and Necker found themselves unable to do much in the way of staving off disaster.

69. THE ECONOMIC SITUATION

The precarious state of the government induced a somewhat dismal interest in things economic. Large international enterprises were forming, the French were in India and commerce extended into far-off lands. There was scarcely an industrial revolution, for machinery had not yet entered the field, but there was a great deal of interest in theoretical economics under the influence of Adam Smith and others of the English school. The favorite topics were the nature of wealth and its distribution. Land as the form of riches was the question taken up by a group known as Physiocrats. It was natural that agriculture should come into its own. As a matter of fact, certain nobles returned to their estates and there engaged in the study of agronomy, in which laudable pursuit they read quantities of manuals produced for that purpose.

There was constantly in the air the feeling that the traditional mode of life was about to change. The word *revolution* even occurred, though not obviously applicable to the existing predicament. Politics were discussed everywhere, in the clubs, the " coffee houses " (newly formed on the English model), in the *côteries*, recently assembled for conversations of serious intent. The prospect of change was felt to apply not merely to government but to the entire social structure and no province was exempt. Society and all connected with it were subjected to scrutiny, or better, to speculative thought.

70. THE PHILOSOPHERS

All these subjects, with natural science added, were appropriated by the " Philosophes." Here is a label difficult to define: Marivaux (1688–1763) was essentially a writer of refined comedy of " spiderweb " structure,[1] although he did also a certain amount of propaganda in the *Ile des Esclaves;* Montesquieu wrote (1689–1755) on history, politics, and æsthetics; D'Alembert was first and foremost a mathematician, but of broad interests, as shown in his *Discours préliminaire* to the *Encyclopédie* (1751) wherein he attempts to relate the arts and sciences; others (Cadet, Macquer) were natural scientists, yet they were bulked together as Philosophes, when portrayed in the satiric plays of the eighteenth century. " A Philosophe now might be any person allied to or in sympathy with the *Encyclopédie* or a savant interested in any branch of science, or merely a man of letters."[2] Add to the list of genuine notables a horde of *Philosophes à la mode,* that is to say, half-baked, amateurish triflers with all known or knowable things, and the confusion is heightened.

The growth of scientific experimentation led to the appearance of Lavoisier, the great chemist and discoverer of oxygen, with his creation of a completely new chemical nomenclature that amounted to a new chemical language (e.g., " ferrous oxide "). In 1758, an adaptation of the Linnæan system was applied in biology. As far as science is concerned, neology was created into a methodical procedure and the formation of a vocabulary along the model indicated was thenceforth taken for granted.

[1] Cf. Nitze & Dargan, p. 428.
[2] Wade, *Philosophe in Fr. Drama,* p. 130.

71. PRINTING

Printing assumed a position of commercial importance, not only in France, but in Holland, where many " forbidden " books found a medium of publication. The spread of cheap printing meant that such writings were broadcast far and wide, despite the censorship. The specialized terminology belonging to those fields was brought to the attention of a large public. M. Brunot devotes two volumes to the eighteenth century accretions alone. It is therefore impossible to give, in our short space, more than one or two examples from each domain: Politics: *autonomie, patriotisme, antipatriotique;* economics: *transportable, richesses de consommation* vs. *richesses de durée, numéraire;* agriculture and agricultural theory: *agromanie, faire jeûner les arbres, Physiocrate;* commerce: *commercial;* philosophy: *critère, psychologie, sceptique.* No account is here taken of the extensions of sense or metaphors that grew up around these very words.

72. THE " STYLE NOBLE "

With such varied publication, the province of belles-lettres was not as easy to define as in the last century. Where, as in the *conte philosophique,* literature (in the narrow sense) met with philosophy, their vocabularies might join. Voltaire, even here, would be more sparing in neologisms, but others, wherever the chance offered itself, turned their prose into pseudo-scientific gibberish. A poet of the day, Abbé Delille (1738–1813), adopted several horticultural words in his *Jardins,* which are lyric poems, or at least are so classified. The conservative traditional genres, like the tragedy, remained as aloof as ever to any inroads. In fact, as defense reaction, hatred for the expressive word became greater and the circumlocution was more than ever in favor. It was not wise to name the dog on the stage; it was better to call him " *de la fidélité respectable soutien.*" Ducis, who adapted Shakespeare to the taste of his time, had to soften that bard's direct manner and speak of the police in *Othello* as " ces mortels dont l'état gage la vigilance." [3] Rivarol, of whom we shall have occasion to speak in another connection, blamed Voltaire's use of *cordonnier* even in a satire, where some liberty of speech might be expected. Delille, who even boasted of his ingenuity in handling technical terms in his *Jardins* and who might

[3] *Nyrop, Gr. hist.* § 73.

have been suspected of not being hostile to the *mot propre*, felt called upon to substitute *narines* for *naseaux*, apropos of a horse. The "style noble" required the inflation of trivialities. It was necessary that the possibly too direct be made devious and even the remotely obscene be clothed in veils, through which, however, one could see sufficiently well, after the manner of the time, when it was considered the thing to do to clothe "*les sujets les plus scabreux dans un langage irréprochable,*"[4] Even a writer on natural history, the celebrated Buffon, "ennobled" his style. Scientific works so conceived could and did find ready access to the salons. This was the day when, as the saying went, "Newton replaced *Le Grand Cyrus*" on the tables of the great ladies.

73. ROUSSEAU AND BERNARDIN DE SAINT-PIERRE

The first real advance in the art of prose was made during this period by two men, J. J. Rousseau (1712–1778) and Bernardin de Saint-Pierre (1737–1814). The former, always eloquent, at times purely oratorical, possessed altogether new resources that forecast a different era — that of the subjective element in nature, the intermingling of the external and internal worlds. More than that, Rousseau was a musician and his sense of rhythm and harmony was applied to his style; "... *en un temps où le vers ne savait plus chanter, il a orchestré sa prose avec éclat,*" says Lanson.[5] Even Bossuet, whose ear was so keen, did not attain the varied combinations that are striking in the lyric passages of Jean-Jacques, though, of course Bossuet's range of concepts was more limited in the nature of the case. With Bernardin de Saint-Pierre came the *phrase pittoresque*, the type that is *sensation pure, sensation des yeux ou émotion de peintre traduite en formes et en couleurs.*"[6] The jolt suffered by literature in its contacts with other domains was sufficient to make certain alterations in its physiognomy. The shock of contact with the emotion of Rousseau or of Bernardin was the beginning of an entire change in its linguistic resources. What the effects were will be discussed in the next chapter.

Also suggesting the future is the lenient attitude toward dialect in literature, visible in lower genres, such as the peasant comedy of the *Théâtre de la Foire*. While this savors of Marie Antoinette's

---

[4] Cf. Brunot, VI, 103, where also a large list of periphrases is given.
[5] *Art de la prose*, p. 201.
[6] *Ibid.*, p. 204.

Trianon dairy, it gives the peasant, at the same time, perhaps under the impulse of new humanitarian ideals, a prominence hitherto unknown. We are not dealing with the broad comedy of Molière and Dancourt; the " dialect " is not spoken for the same purpose. It is no less the creation of people who know nothing of real patois. The point of interest is that the audience's reaction is not laughter but sentimental sympathy. A ditty of Favart's, *Amours de Bastien et Bastienne* (1753), runs as follows:

> Pourqu'il eût tout l'avantage
> A la fête du hamiau
> De ribans à tout étage
> J'ons embelli son chapiau,
> D'eune gentille rosette
> J'ons orné son flageolet :
> Malgré moi l'ingrat me plaît,
> Faut-il qu'eune autre l'engage
> Après tout ce que j'ai fait ?

to which the critic La Harpe notes: " *Jamais la nature dans toute sa simplicité de la vie champêtre n'a rien inspiré de plus vrai, de plus tendre, de plus gracieux.*" [7] Even the fact that it seems to parody a contemporary play, Rousseau's *Devin du village*, does not destroy the sentimental atmosphere.[8]

74. " GRAMMAIRE RAISONNÉE "

We have seen how the grammarians of Port-Royal codified grammar on logical Cartesian principles. It is clear that the eighteenth century would go further in reacting against Vaugelas and in the direction of more abstract thinking. Vaugelas, to one critic,

... était dans les langues ce que sont dans les sciences les physiciens qui n'ont dans la tête que des faits isolés, et qui les examinent pièce à pièce, sans jamais les soumettre à des vues générales. Même quand il trouve la vérité, il ne donne jamais l'art de la découvrir dans d'autres circonstances; c'est qu'il n'était que grammairien sans être philosophe, et c'est vouloir être astronome sans géometrie.[9]

This passage is significant in showing what happened when the Philosophes took hold of grammar proper. Language was considered,

---

[7] *Chefs d'œuvre classiques*, V, 5–6.
[8] Cf. Lénient, *Comédie au 18e siècle*, II, 208.
[9] François, p. 900.

following the disciples of Locke, as a vehicle for the expression of thought and was therefore to be analyzed in the same manner as one analyzed the processes of thought. " *Jamais les langues n'avaient été considérées de si haut*," writes François.[10] Condillac, prince of *raisonneurs*, states the properties of a verb as being " *de signifier, non pas l'affirmation, mais la coexistence.*" [11]   The application of such grammar to elementary instruction lay in showing the pupil how to " reason " about language, as Dumarsais advocated ." [12] Reasoning often went so far that one forgot the existence of a concrete language with a structure characterized by the existence of certain clear facts. Those facts were at times blissfully disregarded, especially if they interfered with the free play of logic and ran counter to preconceived schemes.

Why stop, indeed, at the analysis of French ? Beauzée, who wrote grammatical articles for the *Encyclopédie*, published in 1767 a *Grammaire générale ou exposition raisonnée des éléments nécessaires du langage, pour servir de fondement à l'étude de toutes les langues.* The last phrase means that the intention was to apply the *raisonneur* methods to general linguistics. Here was something new, which not even Ménage had been able to conceive in the preceding century. Unfortunately, this handling of language in the aggregate, which has nowadays produced such good results, did not reach its fruition in the eighteenth century, for, instead of applying historical principles and seeking what did happen, one substituted speculation as to what must or may have happened. In other words, the origins of language were discussed with the same nonchalance as the origins of society. Rousseau put in his word on language, and his theories were of the wildest. Yet even he aided in bringing attention to linguistics as a science rather than as a mere subject for utilitarian discussion relating to contemporary usage. In that way, the direction was indicated for the development of modern philology. Court de Gébelin, in his *Monde primitif analysé et comparé avec le monde moderne,* spent a great deal of time on the relationships of languages and even planned an etymological dictionary, the first projected, apparently, since Ménage. With all the absurdities of Court de Gébelin, salient traits valuable for the future show conspicuously. The late eighteenth century was overfond of stressing the importance of the Celtic substratum in the formation of modern

[10] *Loc. cit.*
[11] *Op. cit.,* p. 912.
[12] *Ibid.,* p. 903.

French, yet one sees the foundations being laid for progress made in the nineteenth century. Certain scholars were working specially on Old French: La Curne de Sainte-Palaye (1697–1781) prepared a *Dictionnaire historique de l'ancien langage françois ou glossaire de la langue françoise depuis son origine jusqu'au siècle de Louis XIV*, a work on a grand scale, provided even with etymologies, despite which it remained unpublished until 1875. The famous *Aucassin et Nicolette* was published under the title *Amours du bon vieux temps* (1756); and the first edition of the *Ordene de Chevalerie* was that of Barbazan in 1759. The Benedictine order, scholars of long standing, began their immense *Histoire littéraire de la France*, now in its thirty-sixth volume, and being carried on by the *Académie des Inscriptions*. This is a literary project, but its antiquarian aspect later comes to fruition in linguistic research as well.

This book is a history of the northern French language, yet it is not amiss to mention the interest that, at the time of which we speak, arose in the troubadours and their language, in the first place, because research in the southern tongue can hardly be dissociated from the northern, and because the public interest in the national literary past was not clearly defined. Thus we mention in the same paragraph the first serious history of troubadour literature, that of Millot [13] and the far different type of older poetry that has been given the name of the *genre troubadour*. The attempt was, in the latter, to appeal to the current sentimentality about the *bon vieux temps* by aping as well as they knew how — which was none too well — the *style marotique* or whatever it was that they knew of the past. [14]

75. FRENCH ABROAD

The eighteenth century marked the high point in the spread of French abroad. Its most striking popularity was in Germany, from the accession of Frederick II in 1740. That monarch, who rejected his mother tongue in favor of the polished speech of a country politically hostile, used his personal prestige to strengthen French. The Berlin Academy was reconstituted by him; a Frenchman, Maupertuis, presided over it and many a foreigner was found in its ranks. The proceedings were in French and remained so, despite the pro-German reaction, as late as 1804. Frederick's correspond-

[13] *Hist. litt. des troub.*, 1774.
[14] Cf. Baldensperger, *Etudes*, p. 110.

ence with Voltaire and others shows a considerable mastery of the language. Other notable Germans wrote French with purity and delicacy. We notice this even somewhat later, in the correspondence of the Schlegels during the Romantic period. In 1762, observes Nyrop, Moses Mendelssohn remarked that French had been on the verge of becoming the " language of the Berliners." The philosopher and mathematician, Leibnitz, wrote his *Théodicée* in French, but his works are also in Latin and German. In 1784, the Berlin Academy offered a prize for the best essay on the following questions: What has made the French language universal? Why does it deserve that position? Is it likely that it will retain its prestige? At first the prize was awarded to J. C. Schwab, a German professor of the Caroline Academy in Stuttgart. At the insistence of the king, however, the prize was divided with the picturesque, even brilliant, Rivarol. The latter was a southerner, of Italian origin, with apparently noble connections, despite later satires, and despite the fact that his father was at one time obliged to become an innkeeper.[15]   Schwab's methodical dissertation, *Über den Ursachen der Allgemeinheit der französischen Sprache und der wahrscheinlichen Dauer ihrer Herrschaft*, has a strange counterpart in the improvised but brilliant treatment of Rivarol. Of the two, the less scientific but more striking essay is the more durable and its phrase " ce qui n'est pas clair n'est pas français " is quoted often today.[16]

What holds for Germany is true in other lands. Catherine II invited many a distinguished Frenchman to visit Russia. The fact that, on the death of Voltaire, she bought his library, still in Leningrad, is evidence of her enthusiasm. Linguistically, France dominated Italy. The Academy of Turin admitted French into its proceedings in 1759. Abbé Galiani, ambassador of an Italian court, shed tears when he was obliged to go home. Viennese nobility found things French, including the language, decidedly to its taste. Yet it was not the political power of the French government that maintained the influence of the language. On the contrary, Louis XV had little enough prestige in Europe, especially after the disastrous treaty of 1763, when the colonial empire of Louis XIV was lost to England. As Fontenelle wrote to Gottsched, a critic of the French language and of its power, it is only the fact that assiduous cultivation made French a fitting instrument for the adequate

---

[15] Sainte-Beuve, *Causeries du lundi*, V, 62.

[16] For a very readable account of this essay contest and the winners, see Baldensperger, *op. cit.*, p. 1.

expression of ideas that rendered it able to maintain so secure a hold on European civilization.[17]

A reaction is to be observed at the very height of glory. At the death of Frederick II in 1786 one can see a change in feeling. Lessing's *Hamburgische Dramaturgie* is a reaction against literary theory from the other side of the Rhine and also a protest against the linguistic hegemony. In Italy, Alfieri's *Misogallo* sets the pace for a reversion of opinion. The literary " discovery " of Dante and Shakespeare attracts attention in England and Italy to their expressiveness and in France also shows up the lack of vocabulary resources in their translators. The English middle classes become hostile to all that comes from France. An official expression is the bill of March 4, 1732, excluding the vestiges of French from the courts. It is to be noted that the Channel Islands were not affected and French is to this day the language of the legal documents, as we shall have occasion to note later. Inversely, we find in France a wave of Anglomania. It is not within our scope to discuss here the visit of Voltaire to the British Isles and to note the literary manifestations of British influence. Politics, on the contrary, equally important, deserves comment in so far as the lexicon receives such importations as *bill, comité (committee), corporation, excise, budget.* More numerous than items of this category are those referring to English ways of life: *jockey, punch, rosbif (roast beef), redingote, whist.* Exoticisms enter through the intermediary of English: *antilope, chimpanzee, albatross, tomahawk.* Among commercial or transport terms we may list: *drawback, dumping, bushel, whiskey, macadam, chelin (shilling).* An interesting military word, which may have been of ephemeral existence, is *buffetier,* meant to be *beefeater.*

76. LINGUISTIC DIVISION OF FRANCE

What was the situation of the official language in the interior of France ? It is paradoxical that at a time when French was considered " universal " in Europe, it was far from the language of all of Louis XV's subjects. Up to the Revolution, in fact, despite the efforts of Turgot to improve transportation, communications were poor. There were large areas that remained eccentric. Patois was still paramount with many individuals and entire communities, to say nothing of borderlands, where Basque, Flemish and Breton were

[17] *Ibid.,* p. 25.

spoken as they had been for centuries; or recently annexed territories like Alsace, where small inroads had been made on German. In the latter province, the fault was that of the government itself, whose indifference was complete. Political unification satisfied the monarchy. Linguistic unity was a matter of little or no concern.

THE REVOLUTIONARY PERIOD

77. STRIVING FOR UNITY

The word *nation* came into its own with the Revolution. Patriotism became a religion with its appropriate ceremonies recalling those of the church.[18] With a nation so united by a cult, it was declared that the language of a people, *une et indivisible*, forming the republic, had to be likewise one and indivisible, a principle that was the logical precursor of President Wilson's policy of basing political self-determination on linguistic grounds. However, there were practical difficulties with the dialectal situation, as we have said. These were brought into the limelight by the questionnaire of a member of the Convention, Abbé Grégoire, which showed that the extent and gravity of the situation was far greater than imagined. Progress was made by the growth of national feeling, especially during the invasions, but the real solution of the patois question could not be attained even by the most drastic measures of the Terror, the agents of which could do nothing but fulminate against the refractory peasants who could not give up their dialect overnight and adopt good Parisian in the wink of an eye. The Revolutionary Convention felt that those regions, like the Basque territory or Brittany, that did not speak French were the stamping grounds of counterrevolutionary movements and their zeal in suppressing them was great; greater, it may be said, than their ultimate success.[19]

[18] See, for an instance of a revolutionary celebration, the illustration facing page 152 of Bédier-Hazard, *Hist. de la litt. française;* also Brunot's Chapter II (T. IX, p. 2): " *Caractère religieux de la révolution* " and p. 901, bottom.

[19] Cf. Febvre. *op. cit.* Brunot shows that it was a French song, composed at Strasbourg, which was adopted by the southerners and called the Marseillaise (IX, pt. 1, p. 71). Such events could not fail to inspire at least the desire to learn the language of the Republic.

78. RELATIVE CONSERVATISM OF THE REVOLUTION

One is tempted to ascribe to the official tongue deep-seated changes commensurate with those taking place in the body politic. It is true that a new political jargon arises: *Ci-devant* aristocrats are tried for *incivisme*. There are *Jacobins* whose creed is saddled with an *–isme*. A new calendar is manufactured out of whole cloth; so is a new system of measures, the metric system. Political consciousness draws in thousands of citizens. Purism suffers a blow in the suppression of the salons, and the Academy is closed. These changes are superficial. Political thought is largely limited to the bourgeoisie. The demagogue in truth often feels called upon to *parler peuple* and, as Brunot and Bruneau express it, " *Une vague de vulgarité, de scatologie, d'ordure déferle.*" [20] It is curious to note that the royalists were as guilty as certain revolutionaries and that such republicans as Desmoulins and Marat opposed the practice of " talking down " to the people, trained as these leaders were in the traditions of the old regime, i.e., on principles that satisfy oratorical needs. The puristic principles, if they were not conducive to lyricism, did contribute to eloquence. Throughout the Revolution, the *Journal de la langue française tant exacte qu'ornée*, founded by Domergue in 1784 to maintain the classic ideals in language and the canons of *grammaire générale et raisonnée*, not only maintained itself but virtually took over the linguistic functions of the suppressed Academy. The last flourish of the academic trumpet was still to be sounded with the Girault-Duviviers *Grammaire des grammaires* during the Restoration (1818).

79 A. PHONETIC CHANGES

For a century, the imperfect and conditional ending *–ois* [wɛ] had been tending toward [ɛ]. Voltaire (1694–1778) recommended in the preface to the edition of the tragedy *Zaïre* (published 1736) that it be written *–ais* to conform to its pronunciation (cf. also *Discours sur les Welches*). His reform was not accepted until the sixth edition of the Academy dictionary, 1835, and even then there was left an anomalous situation where we have *anglais* on the one hand and *suédois* on the other. At the same time the existing diphthong [wɛ] had been evolving since the fifteenth century toward [wa] among the common people of Paris. In the eighteenth century

[20] *Gr. Hist.* Introduction, p. xxxi.

even conservative grammarians began to allow this common pronunciation in monosyllables *pois, bois,* etc. The fact was that [wɛ] by this time was greatly restricted in use, limited, in fact, to court aristocracy. When the members of that class were submerged during the Revolution, their pronunciation went with them. That certain of the older generation kept their speech habits is shown by the case of Lafayette, who, on his visit to the United States in 1824, still pronounced *le roi* as [lərwɛ]. During the eighteenth century by school influence the final *r* was gradually restored in *-ir* infinitives. It was also pronounced once more in the suffix *-eur* and in certain individual words. Final *l* also reappeared in *il, péril,* and a few other cases.

We may list, in conclusion, several eighteenth century dictionaries, with the major reforms indicated by each: In general, the *Dictionnaire de Trévoux* (first edition 1704) is inspired by Furetière and the encyclopedia tendencies; it leans toward a liberal policy in the admission of words. The second, or 1718 edition of the Academy dictionary, is of no importance beyond the adoption of the alphabetical order. The 1740 version (edited by Abbé d'Olivet) includes important spelling reforms: removal of unpronounced *s* + consonant, e.g. *be(s)tise, i(s)le:* removal of *e* in *sc(e)u* and *d(e)u.* The edition of 1762, besides showing greater leniency toward neologism, takes greater care in the separation of the *lettres ramistes, u, v, i, j.* The Revolution produced its results in the 1798 dictionary, which was nothing but that of 1762 plus a supplement of 336 Revolutionary words, the product, principally, of the Terror, 1793–94. This version was later repudiated by the Academy.

79 B. EIGHTEENTH CENTURY TRANSLATION

Ayant entendu, dans la grande salle, un vacarme horrible, qui sembloit provenir d'une bête sauvage qui s'en vouloit échapper, nous nous occupâmes d'en savoir la cause. On trouva Eumolpe, retiré dans un coin, qui remplissoit un très-grand parchemin de ses vers. Tout étonnés que nous fussions de voir une personne qui n'avoit point envie de quitter les Muses, même devant le danger de mort, nous nous emparâmes de lui, qui se démenoit, cependant, comme un possédé, et nous l'engageâmes de se rendre à la raison. Il faut croire que la Raison étoit pour fort peu dans la tête de ce rimeur, qui crioit: « Laissez-moi finir ces vers, car ce n'est pas une chose aisée de les achever. » Pour ma part, je mis main forte sur ce drôle et je priois Dione de le transporter, tant bien que mal, sur terre.

REFERENCES

ALEXIS, F., *La langue postclassique* (Vol. VI of Brunot's *Histoire*, Part II. Paris: A. Colin, 1905).

BALDENSPERGER, F., *Études d'histoire littéraire.* (Paris: Hachette, 1907). p.l.: *Comment le 18ᵉ siècle expliquait l'universalité de la langue française.* p. 110: *Le "genre troubadour."*

BEHRENS, D., *Ueber Engl. Sprachgut im Franz.*, (Giessen, 1927).

BRUNETIÈRE, F., *Les transformations de la langue française au 18ᵉ siècle*, in *Rev. D. Mondes*, XXX (1905), 336–368.

CAVALLIERE, A., " Rivarol e la filosofia del linguaggio nel 700," in *Archiv. rom.*, XVIII (1934), 567.

FEBVRE, L., " Langue et nationalité en France au 18ᵉ siècle," in *Revue de synthèse historique*, XLII (1926), 22.

FREY, MAX., *Les transformations du vocabulaire français à l'époque de la Révolution.* (Paris: Presses Univ. de France, 1925).

GOHIN, F., *Les transformations de la langue française de 1740 à 1789* (Paris: Belin frères, 1903).

JEANROY, A., *Les études provençales du XVIᵉ siècle au milieu du XIXᵉ* (Paris, Toulouse: Privat, 1931).

PEYRE, H., *La royauté et les langues provinciales* (Paris: Presses modernes, 1933).

WADE, I. O., *The "Philosophe" in the French Drama of the 18th Century* (Princeton: Univ. Press; Paris: Presses Univ. de France, 1926).

IX

THE NINETEENTH CENTURY

80. HISTORICAL SITUATION

At the opening of the century, the *Directoire* becomes a Consulate and the Consulate soon turns into an Empire. Napoleon I endeavors to establish a new nobility, but this new aristocracy, recruited often from the masses, does not constitute a cultural elite. The emperor himself is of middle estate and a foreigner besides. The cultural type of the revolutionary demagogues, provided with a solid classical education, does not appear conspicuously in Napoleon's reign. There is little chance for eloquence, throttled by the censorship. The head of the government, a Corsican, is not concerned with the finesses of the French tradition. In primary education there is no interest at all; that of the girls is left altogether to the family. The creation of the *lycée* and the administrative centralization of the schools works advantageously for education, but the curriculum does not share in the general advance, at least as far as French is concerned. Latin is more firmly entrenched than ever. The people at large are not in a mood to react strongly to any educational policy. The aftermath of great victories and crushing disasters produces a general apathy. Most of the vocabulary added during the Revolution is either subtly altered or laughed at. As far as grammar is concerned, the ghost of the recently departed M. Domergue, respected editor of the *Journal de la langue française*, haunts the editors and authors of textbooks and these grammarians reason logically, in tune with their times, as we shall have occasion to see.

81. FORCES OF CHANGE

From abroad there comes a vivifying breath. Mme de Staël upsets the imperial police and her *De l'Allemagne* threatens the complacency with which traditional æsthetic concepts are regarded. Chateaubriand's sachems and tomahawks become literary baggage.

Their use, it is true, appears like that of mere brilliant patches, conspicuously external, which do not materially affect the traditional foundations of structure. Yet there is danger to classical prejudices in Chateaubriand's love of neologism, his abhorrence of the periphrase and his inclination toward the *mot propre*, which despite a lingering fondness for " rubber stamps " of the " alabaster neck " type, nevertheless shows in his prose, along with a wealth of color terms, rare in the classic writers and inherited from such as Bernardin de Saint-Pierre.[1]

82. LINGUISTICS IN THE EIGHTEENTH AND NINETEENTH CENTURIES

Among the scholars, things were happening fast. In the eighteenth century the struggle of the British and French for the possession of India had attracted attention to Sanskrit. During Napoleon's regime Champollion deciphered the Rosetta Stone and gave the impetus to all future Egyptian studies. Although Germany, before and during the French Revolution, had stolen a march on France by developing research in comparative linguistics, Paris, during the Empire, was becoming a mecca for all those interested in the historical approach to the study of language. Not only Oriental and classical manuscripts were found and studied, but Old French and Provençal as well. Many famous Germans came to work in the national libraries of France, among them the Schlegels (August and Wilhelm) and Tieck. A large number of these German scholars were Romantic poets and as such were imbued with the spirit of the Middle Ages. Soon there grew up an analogous type of French scholar-poet. Raynouard (1761–1856), a southern lawyer, wrote a blood-and-thunder tragedy called *Les Templiers*, the title of which is sufficiently significant of his interest in the Middle Ages. He explored the manuscripts that dealt with the language of his native Midi and edited many of them, uncritically, to be sure. He imagined the language of the troubadours to be a *langue romane* intermediate between Latin and Romance, falling in line with a tendency of his time to consider Sanskrit as intermediate between Indo-European and the tongues of modern Europe. While his *Grammaire romane* (1819), wherein those theories were expounded, is no longer valid, his dictionary, or *Lexique roman* (1838–1844), is still useful enough to have been recently reprinted. In our Intro-

[1] Mornet, *Hist. de la clarté française.*, p. 344.

duction we mentioned Friedrich Diez, who, following the methods of the comparativists, founded the comparative grammar of the Romance languages. His procedure meant doing away, for the time being, with purely national viewpoints and with those considerations which proceeded from the notion of a " racial genius " and a " racial taste." As far as a theory of fixity of language is concerned, it meant that the classical period was at an end.

83. LINGUISTS AND *LITTÉRATEURS*

The manner in which the new concepts found their way into purely literary channels has yet to be studied in detail. The philologic tradition was old, but it was in the nineteenth century, through scholarly men like Fauriel (1772–1844) and through remarkable amateurs like Nodier (1780–1844), that Victor Hugo and his associates became impressed with the mobility and flux of language. These names, Fauriel and especially Nodier, have unfortunately become associated with a kind of superficial learning, but they by no means deserve the patronizing smiles that many have seen fit to bestow upon them. Their function was to interest the public in the historical method as they focused attention on the national past. Fauriel was a professor at the Sorbonne, but his lectures drew a wider range of auditors than usual. He had the gift of rendering attractive his discourses on the Old French epic or on Old Provençal. His breadth of interest was great; some say too great to be accurate: he translated from Italian poets and novelists; he prepared an Old Provençal dictionary, still unpublished and stowed away in a cardboard box at the *Bibliothèque de l'Institut*, with other personal papers. He was socially popular and interested the *beau monde* in his work. Nodier was a more versatile if also a more superficial person; journalist under Napoleon I, newspaper editor in Illyria, entomologist, amateur philologist, librarian, he had the gift, if not of originating ideas, of transmitting them to the people he attracted to his salons in the back rooms of the Arsenal Library, of which he was custodian. Here gathered the famous *premier cénacle*, on whom Nodier impressed his views, queer and sound. So it happens that, if we find in Victor Hugo's *Préface de Cromwell* a tirade against the classic gentlemen who would but could not stop linguistic evolution and who, like literary Joshuas, cause the sun to stand still, we may trace it back to types like Fauriel and Nodier, intermediaries between philologists and pure literati. From such a source

Victor Hugo drew encouragement, if indeed he needed any. Besides encouragement, in theory, Victor Hugo felt he had for his interest in archaic, dialectal, and craft terms an illustrious precedent in Ronsard, buried since the first quarter of the seventeenth century and disinterred by the indefatigable Sainte-Beuve in search of a pedigree for the nascent Romanticism. Let us point out that Ronsard offers more interest to us as a parallel than as ancestor to Victor Hugo's philologic proclivities. Both he and the chief of the Pléiade lived right after, if not during, a development of the research spirit; Ronsard was in a sense the heir of Guillaume Budé and was the pupil of the scholar Daurat, while Hugo was the heir, in the same sense, of the Revolutionary linguistic group.

84. ART AND HUMANITY

If we would play with words in the manner of Hugo, we might say that the term *human* occurs as key word in the *humanistic* Renaissance of the sixteenth century and in the *humanitarian* movement for which Herder in Germany, Rousseau, and the author of *Les Misérables* stood. Social transformation is a necessary concomitant of linguistic change in the profounder sense, because words mean ideas and change with them. It is therefore not astonishing to see a social change accompanied by a vocabulary revolution. Add to the purely human angle the question of the attitude toward nature as demonstrated by Rousseau and Bernardin de Saint-Pierre, and we can realize what a new stream enters the current of nineteenth-century thought, with wild and colorful landscapes replacing the white of classic thought. The subject matter and the person are one with the vehicle of transmission. Buffon had already said " *Le style c'est l'homme même.*" Rousseau refused to subject his personal style to puristic standards, believing it to be necessary for him to express himself with freedom. These men laid the foundation of the nineteenth-century conception of prose, founded on art, but intimately associated with things human and conceived from the angle of the individual, differing thus from that of the seventeenth century, in its main lines.

The role of emotion, under such circumstances, must of necessity loom large. The *culte du moi*,[2] with its strenuous lyricism, called for the *mot frissonnant* to express the nuances of feeling. The old correct but poor vocabulary, the *gueuse fière* of classic times, now

---

[2] Vossler, p. 362.

appeared to the nineteenth century merely as a *gueuse*, a beggar, without any social graces.

Although Chateaubriand had already voiced his consciousness of being an innovator, it was some time before the actual Romantic revolt was conceived in linguistic terms. In 1823, Lamartine explicitly separated Romantic thought from any possible revolutionary technique in expression: " *Classique pour l'expression, romantique dans la pensée; à mon avis c'est ce qu'il faut être.*"[3] At the same time, Stendhal wondered how anybody could write a good tragedy minus two-thirds of the spoken language. In the early twenties, therefore, one may note a difference of attitude within the Romantic school.

85. THE CONSERVATIVE FORCES

It is probable that the battle would have been put off for some time if the conservatives had not forced the issue. In grammar, the disciples of Lhomond, Restaut, and the eighteenth-century *raisonneurs*, continued to reason out rules that it was impossible to follow and which, it was soon noticed, were not actually being followed, even by their proponents. When the disciples of Domergue lost their leader, they adopted the grammar of Noël and Chapsal (1823), which reigned long as the supreme authority, underwent innumerable editions and, in some form or other, still haunts the quays along the Seine. In the name of these and similar grammarians, edicts more and more tyrannical issued forth from the classic fortresses (the term is Brunot's). In the domain of literary vocabulary, proclamations of like nature went so far as to attack the use of *parfois* in an epic, on the ground that it was trivial. The last straw was furnished by the periphrase makers,[4] of whom we had heard in the eighteenth century and who were working industriously in the nineteenth. In the celebrated *Préface de Cromwell* (1827), Victor Hugo attacked the school of Delille with its horror of the direct and vigorous. The muse of that famous abbé was so prudish that it would find fault with Corneille,[5] " *et il a fallu bien des seigneur ! et bien des madame! pour faire pardonner à notre admirable Racine ses chiens si monosyllabiques . . .*" Hugo was not a bit impressed with the " nobility " of the neoclassic manner as practiced by con-

[3] P. de Julleville, VIII, 709.
[4] *Ibid.*, p. 729.
[5] Ed. Effinger, p. 92.

temporaries: " *En somme, rien n'est si* commun *que cette élégance et cette noblesse de convention . . . Des idées d'emprunt vêtues d'images de pacotille.*" With Hugo the barriers were lowered to permit the entry of dialect, archaism, and the technology of arts and crafts, to say nothing of argot, the slang of the galley slaves and of the world of the urchin Gavroche. Reviewing his own accomplishments, he said in his " Réponse à un acte d'accusation " (*Contemplations,* I, § 7):

> Les mots, bien ou mal nés, vivaient parqués en castes;
> Les uns, nobles, hantant les Phèdres, les Jocastes,
> Les Méropes, ayant le décorum pour loi,
> Et montant à Versaille aux carosses du roi;
> Les autres, tas de gueux, drôles patibulaires,
> Habitant les patois, quelques-uns aux galères
> Dans l'argot; dévoués aux genres bas
> . . . .
> Alors, brigand, je vins, je m'écriai: " Pourquoi
> Ceux-ci, toujours devant, ceux-là toujours derrière? "
> . . . .
> Je mis un bonnet rouge au vieux dictionnaire.
> Plus de mot sénateur! plus de mot roturier;
> . . . .
> Je nommai le cochon par son nom; pourquoi pas?
> J'ôtai du cou du chien stupéfait son collier
> D'épithètes. . . .

the last phrase being an allusion to his liking for the *mot propre* and his hate for the elaborate periphrase.

He was too much of an artist to let himself go entirely. Yet because of his temperament, he reveled in verbal virtuosity; many a passage is a welter of paradox and antithesis; the chapter in *Notre Dame* called " Paris à vol d'oiseau " must be almost incomprehensible to the reader unacquainted with the architectural terminology of the late Middle Ages. That is what Hugo called "*faire vrai,*" but it was his own conception of reality, or, if one will, reality conceived through the *culte du moi.* This cult of self-expression was at first conservative, in that the Romantics who were its high priests in the main respected the classic syntax, but the principles of individual liberty, once laid down, were to be productive of change even after the Romantic movement had run its course.

86. BALZAC

With Honoré de Balzac (1799–1850), the realistic movement is entrenched. The scope of literary endeavor is enlarged so that it includes many fields previously excluded. Balzac, at one time, was concerned with business, and his fantastic commercial projects, although finding nothing but a ludicrous end in failure, lived on in his mind and were exploited in his novels, clothed in all their trade jargon. With Rabelaisian encyclopedism, he prided himself on a considerable familiarity with numerous specialties. " There are three of us in Paris," said he, " who know our language, Hugo, Gautier and I," and he meant that these three had a wide vocabulary which it was their duty to contribute, like alms, to the impoverished French tongue. Balzac's store of terms is so great that a separate glossary is necessary to read him with accuracy. Besides the archaisms, neologisms or exoticisms that we have noted in his predecessors, the natural sciences, the financial world, peasant life, and the underworld find linguistic representation. Balzac uses in his " crook " novels (e.g., *La dernière incarnation de Vautrin*) even the *largonj* or *loucherbem*, a sort of criminal's " pig Latin," formed by the artificial shifting of letters. Like Rabelais — and like Hugo, for that matter — he becomes intoxicated with words and uses strings of associated terms apparently for the mere pleasure of piling them on. In the *Peau de Chagrin* (p. 32) he uses *farthing, kopeck, creuzer* and *tarain*, i.e., names of coins, in one sentence; and similarly, scientific terms, *asparagine, vauqueline, digitaline,* follow in imposing series. It is not astonishing to find whole pieces, the *Contes drolatiques*, done in the quasi-Rabelais manner which delighted him so hugely. With all his vocabulary, it is not in his form that he shines. It has been remarked that his sentences may not even make sense at all times and Lanson, in his *Art de la Prose*, has little praise for his style, his hasty and often bad composition. That, of course, is not our direct province to discuss. We can summarize Balzac's contribution as that of a verbal virtuoso, dazzling the reader with luxuriant wealth.

87. GAUTIER

Théophile Gautier (1811–1872), red-vested lieutenant of Hugo at the time of *Hernani's* first production, traveler in Spain, interested in things Chinese, used exotic words to flavor his writings on foreign lands. However, more important than this rather obvious point is the manner in which his artistic interests were reflected in his literature. Besides the technical element, taken from the jargon of painting or sculpture or from the general vocabulary of æsthetics, he transferred his interest in the plastic arts to words themselves, considering each word as an uncut stone that could be trimmed and made attractive. Thus Gautier is one of the most important in putting into concrete language the theory of prose that is beautiful and artistic per se. It is true that no exaggerations such as we shall discuss in the next chapter are as yet visible, and the cult of obscurity has not seized him.

88. FLAUBERT

Gustave Flaubert (1821–1880) is more discriminating, perhaps, than any of his predecessors in the realm of prose. We need not repeat how carefully he wrote, how patiently, by speaking his sentences as he wrote them, he tried out with his *gueuloir*, his oral effectiveness. It is more interesting to stress the fact that he did so in the name of the classics, Boileau and Labruyère. "*Je couche avec le* Dictionnaire des dictionnaires," said he, so anxious was he that his word was the *mot juste*, not merely the *mot propre* that had satisfied Hugo. He possessed a large vocabulary; his *Correspondance* is alive with images and terms from the popular strata, with archaisms and coinages, with dialect terms from his native Norman, but he is restrained in his use of them in more formal literature. Of course there is *Salammbô*, a museum of antique words that are difficult enough for the average public, but Flaubert, in the main, did not attempt to browbeat his reader with an avalanche of incomprehensibles. He turned down many a desirable word with the dictum "*ça ne fait pas image au lecteur.*" With the metaphor, the symbolic expression, on the contrary, he played to his heart's content, and his comparisons are of a type unthinkable in the age of Louis XIV, perhaps of a type psychologically in advance of his own time. There have been studies made on his vocabulary and a very careful elaborate one on his imagery, but his syntax has not been the object of an *étude d'ensemble*. Now artistry, in the positive sense, is the hallmark of the nineteenth century. Flaubert, in his conscious striving for the creation of his art form, is of his time, whether it be in his search for the exact word, the use of the imperfect to picture the world of the spirit or his handling of the *style indirect libre* in rendering a conversation vividly without actually quoting. In these devices he moves away from the spoken language and in the direction of a special prose. No radical dislocations of syntax are yet to be recorded, however. In this respect, we must wait for the advent of the Impressionists and the Symbolists.

89. DIALECT IN LITERATURE

In the meantime, let us go back to the beginning of the century in order to study a thin but well-defined current, that of dialectal influence, which we already have suggested. We have seen how, in the theater of the eighteenth century, a change was visible in the attitude toward the peasant. It seems that this greater sympathy was independent of the Romantic movement, for a violent opponent like Paul-Louis Courier portrays the country folk and makes an attempt to create for them a quasi dialect, largely concocted out of Amyot's archaic French.[6] The Swiss, Toeppfer, uses his local patois in his descriptions and short stories as a form of embellishment, believing that " *tous les paysans ont du style.*" Although his dialect is a composite rather than the authentic speech of the Geneva region, we are nevertheless out of the province of purely artificial peasant brogues as they were in the seventeenth century. It is merely a case, at this period, of literature and the literary medium coming in contact with the " *français de souche* " (the expression is Toeppfer's) and being no longer ashamed to admit it.

The new trend finds its major exponent in George Sand (1804–1876). To her, the man of the soil, removed from the " *vie factice,*" has not only a greater feeling for nature but has developed a method of expression commensurate with that feeling. Sand believes that not only is a peasant an artist, but adds, " *je prétends que leur art est supérieur au nôtre.*" The peasant's language is necessary to portray this superior art. It is, however, impossible — and she is not slow to recognize the fact — to confront the " Parisian " reader with an unintelligible speech. Therefore she compromises on a modified form of her central patois, the Berrichon, amply diluted with Parisian or, as it turns out on examination, with archaic French (Amyot, Rabelais, etc.) designed to add quaintness, the effect she apparently desired. The critics (notably one Gustave Planche) who attacked her for using a conventionalized patois are essentially wrong, because the base is clearly Berrichon or, at times,

---

[6] Cf. the *Pétition pour les villageois qu'on empêche de danser.*

the subdialect of La Marche, which we find in stories of which the scene is placed in the *département de la Creuse*. Besides being on the whole fairly genuine, it was effectively presented and the enthusiasm of the public was immense. There is no doubt that this success was instrumental in determining the course of linguistic realism in the nineteenth century and contemporary period. Maupassant, when the occasion demands, has his peasants talk Norman (at times some other dialect), underscoring the words or idioms that might seem strange to the reader. A long string of writers have followed his precedent.

90. ARGOT

The same emphasis along sociological lines brought about the penetration of argot, which, as we have seen, Victor Hugo " rescued from the galleys " and used in *Les Misérables* and (with Guernsey dialect) *Les travailleurs de la mer*. Of Balzac we have spoken sufficiently. The trend increased with the Naturalists. Zola (1840–1902), for instance, laid under heavy contribution Delvau's *Dictionnaire de l'argot*, regarding that as indispensable as his manuals of science, but he poured the crude mass of slang into a finely shaped mold.[7]

91. HISTORICAL FACTORS

It is well, at this point, to stop and look into contemporary history, in order to judge what conditions were forming the new attitude of society, for there had to be a public receptive to this *argot* of the Parisian slums, the patois of Guernsey fishermen or Berry peasants as well as the orientalisms of a Loti or Gautier.

In 1830, the French undertook the conquest of Algeria. With the returning soldiers came a number of Arabic words into current speech, e.g., *zouave*. There is the beginning of a new colonial expansion which will mean contact with Indo-China (1863) and an interest in things Chinese. This is the age of inventions. The coming of the railroads, telegraph, etc., besides filling the spoken and ultimately the literary language with mechanical terms, had a vast influence on the unity of France through the increased penetration of Paris into the provinces and the interpenetration of the dialects

---

[7] The expression is Zola's, "*une moule très travaillée.*" Brunot, in his recent historical grammar (in collaboration with Bruneau) remarks (Introduction, p. XL): "*Du propre aveu de l'auteur, L'Assommoir (1877) est un essai philologique.*"

themselves, thus confusing the phonological drift of each entity. The influence of the official speech was augmented by the creation of a primary public school system under the ægis of the democratically minded Louis-Philippe. The vernacular became a potent factor, assuming greater importance when, in 1865, the secondary system admitted a course without Greek and Latin as absolute requirements.

92. INFLUENCE OF THE IMPRESSIONISTS

To return now to the literary situation. We have noted the relative conservatism of the Romantics and Realists with reference to basic structure. With the Impressionists, there is distortion in the nature of the vocabulary and dislocation of syntax. The reasons for such deep-seated changes lie in the purposes of Impressionism, which include the portrayal of the most fleeting sensations, the most intricate of personal reactions to phenomena, often momentary, of sight, sound and even smell. Conventional definitions are twisted and words from one domain of life brought into another (" warm smells " for instance). The process is of course not new, for Balzac had already spoken of a house which projected a yellow haze into the atmosphere. Such tricks are multiplied by the Goncourt brothers, who also created, for their special needs, a jerky, nervous style, which, if it seemed removed from the old rhythms, had a tempo of its own that suggested instantaneous sensations, quick turns and twists, sudden suggestions. The syntax could not fail to react to the new *écriture artiste:* connectives and *mots-outils* or auxiliary particles had to be reduced to the limit. Picturesque tenses, like the present and the imperfect received renewed vitality; position of adjectives was changed: adjectives were used often as substantives. The general presentation sometimes approached the type of mere notes, especially in pure description, where the economy of phrase paralleled the economy of line to be found in a sketch.

Out of such a sketch, Loti makes pictures in words, real paintings full of color, *chiaroscuro*, lights and darks in *Pêcheur d'Islande*, exotic hues of all kinds in his stories of the South Seas or the Orient. He is obliged to adapt words to new uses: *des roches* criblaient *la mer*, l'étendue *miroite au soleil*. But it is less in his vocabulary than in his style, his strangely timeless verbs, his sentences without verbs, left hanging in the air, that he finds his effects. His prose is *prose d'art* not merely in the sense that it is highly literary and individual but in the sense that it is used to secure the ends of plastic art.

With the poets, linguistic radicalism was naturally carried further. Baudelaire, who believed in sense transference, substituted sounds for colors, colors for odors. Rimbaud wrote a poem about " blue " and " red " vowels. Verlaine, *ivrogne de génie*, had no consciousness of any tradition. " *De la musique avant toute chose*," he exclaimed and preferred therefore the word that sounds well without necessarily being the exact term, a process which, with Mallarmé, readily turns toward obscurity. In the case of Verlaine there was absent that education and discipline necessary to comprehend the true sense of words; especially in his later period he attributes to them meanings undiscoverable in any standard dictionary, meanings that perhaps nobody ever dreamed of but himself in a haze of absinthe. With the Symbolists it may be that the number of foreigners in the group (Moréas, Merrill) tended to reduce the consciousness of the fact that French had a history that antedated the Symbolists, a history very old and very potent in its effects. At the same time let us not forget that these writers, in so far as they were anti-middle class, enjoyed shocking people of classic sympathies and the tactics of *épater le bourgeois* were at the bottom of many audacities.

While all this goes on, we have Renan (1823–1892) and Anatole France (1844–1924), whose sympathies are classic and whose style is elegant and chaste, in the best tradition, clear and beautifully rhythmed. Yet the former, as an archæologist, enjoys the archaic to a considerable extent, and of the latter it has been said that his vocabulary is probably more modern than one thinks from reading the apparently eighteenth-century style that he occasionally affects. At any rate, a thoroughgoing study would most probably reveal facts that would be of more than passing interest and which might even astonish some. Such a study is highly necessary in the case of Anatole France, about whose language we tend to generalize too much.

93. CONSERVATIVE FORCES

It is paradoxical that while literature is in general becoming radical, the forces of conservatism are on the ascendant in the spoken tongue. The newspaper and compulsory military service tend to uniformity of language, to the increasing penetration of correct language into the remotest dialects. Paris being increasingly the source of political preferment and some social distinction, its vernacular acquires a prestige which is certainly a powerful factor in making the peasant ashamed of his patois. In the south, where the dialects are especially alive, many people become bilingual, their French being strongly influenced by their old speech habits. In Paris itself under the Restoration there is a concentration of population and a mixing of classes, the wealthy living on the first floor of a tall house, the bourgeois of medium resources higher up, and the poor in the attic. That is the type of dwelling house pictured in *La Vie de Bohème* or *Sylvestre Bonnard*, where the scholar lives close to the book peddler. That situation, as Dauzat remarks,[8] is temporary, the modern city plan operating in favor of a segregation of industries and social classes in the various districts of the city and suburbs. The theater of the nineteenth century not only spreads its diction over the country but it does so with special effect, as its language is now that of every day. Lastly, the obligatory free school system created by Jules Ferry (1881) brings elementary instruction to the tiniest villages. The system is centralized and the teaching of French standardized. The *baccalauréat* obliges the student to come to his department capital for examination and even to Paris for certain degrees and competitions. In matters of detail, the government imposes uniformity. Spelling and grammar rules are laid down with an authority all the more binding in that the *baccalauréat* diploma is required for many government positions. Thus arises a " bureaucracy of language "[9] which is still in force. To those familiar with the history of the seventeenth century, such control is not surprising. In fact it is entirely within the tradition.

94. ENGLISH INFLUENCE

Throughout the nineteenth century, English exercises great influence on commerce, politics, journalism, and particularly sports in France. Some of the additions are in reality re-imports of words that were once French and, having lived for a certain time on foreign soil, have acquired new characteristics, e.g., Old French *bougette* (small leather sack) which in England became *budget* and was thus brought back to its former land. So it was with Old French *desport, disport,* English *sport; entrevue > interview; étiquette > ticket.* But many, in fact the vast majority, had never seen French soil before

---

[8] *Hist.*, p. 566.
[9] The expression is that of Brunot, *Gr. hist.*

their adoption. Certain Frenchmen viewed the new Anglomania with horror: Musset, in the person of Van Buck, a character of *Il ne faut jurer de rien*, vents his keen satire on the strange-sounding vocables. The eminent critic and author, Rémy de Gourmont (1858–1915) devotes much space in his *Esthétique de la langue française* to what he believes a menace to the essential nature of his mother tongue. It is true, he says, that words must be borrowed. It has been proved by the history of linguistic science, under the leadership of Gaston Paris, whom he is proud to acknowledge his master in that field. Yet English is not the natural reservoir for French borrowings. It is often unpleasant to the ear. The person who crowds numerous foreignisms into his discourse is a new *écolier limousin*. At times English borrowings are ridiculous, as when a rose labeled *Harry Cower* must be read as if it were *haricot vert*.[10] This critic has not hindered the English invasion. We shall see in the next chapter how it is apparent in the contemporary period.

95. DIPLOMACY

As a diplomatic language, French lost some of its prestige after the Franco-Prussian war (1870). English began to acquire a distinct superiority in the realm of business.

96. ROMANCE LINGUISTICS

In one field, French, together with other Romance languages, took on a new importance. We have mentioned the activities of the comparative philologists in the beginning of the century. It was not until the late 1850's that those methods began to be applied to the modern tongue in France, the early part of the period being not consistently productive and even, from 1830 to 1855, quite barren and unscientific. The lexicographer Littré began his dictionary in 1859 and finished it in 1872. This monumental work, a giant task for one man, is still of value, especially for the *Historique* which follows every article and in which examples from the earliest occurrence are listed chronologically. The etymologies, made as they were before the age of phonological discoveries, are untrustworthy. The Renaissance of Romance linguistic studies is due to the venerated Gaston Paris (1839–1903). His work on the function of Latin accent (*Etude sur le rôle de l'accent latin dans la langue*

---

[10] The last is an excellent example of the extremes to which even a person of such taste as R. de Gourmont will go in his hostility.

française) was epoch-making and laid the foundations for phonological research in Romance. In 1872, in collaboration with Paul
Meyer (1840–1917), he began the periodical *Romania*, perhaps the
foremost journal in the field today. The year 1870 had seen the
founding of the *Revue des langues romanes* under Chabaneau, devoted primarily to the language and literature of the south. Gaston
Paris was not afraid to face the criticism of certain of his country-
men in at least starting from the principles and methods current
by this time on the other side of the Rhine, although the personal
stamp, nay even the national character, particularly in the clarity
and attractiveness of his presentation, is far from absent. The procedure of Gaston Paris is still in honor today, but that is a subject
for a subsequent chapter.

REFERENCES

AHLSTRÖM, A., *La langue de Flaubert* (Macon: Protat Frères, 1899).
BASKETT, MARY FRANCES — *Tense usage as a stylistic device in Madame Bovary*, M. A. thesis, Ohio State University, 1933.
BEHRENS, D., " Ueber deutsches Sprachgut im Französischen " in *Giessener Beiträge zur rom. Phil.* (1924).
BRUNOT, F., and BRUNEAU, C., *Précis de grammaire historique de la langue française* (Paris: Masson, 1930).
DEMOREST, D. L., *L'expression figurée et symbolique dans l'œuvre de Flaubert* (Paris: L. Conard, 1931).
GASCHET, H., *Les pastorales de Longus, trad. par P.-L. Courier. Etude critique, suivies d'une étude sur l'essai de style vieilli de Courier* (Paris: Larose et Tenin, 1911).
GOURMONT, R. DE, *Esthétique de la langue française* (Paris: Soc. du Mercure de France, 1899).
LANSON, G., *L'art de la prose* (Paris: Librairie des Annales, 1909).
LOESCH, G., *Die impressionistische Sprache der Goncourts* (Nürnberg: Hilz, 1919).
MORNET, D., *Histoire de la clarté française* (Paris: Payot, 1929).
SCHUTZ, A. H., *Peasant Vocabulary in the Works of George Sand*. Univ. of Missouri Studies, II, I. (Columbia, Mo.: Univ. Press, 1927).
" The philological activity of Charles Nodier," *Studies in Philology*, XXIII (1927), 404.
THIBAUDET, A., *Gustave Flaubert* (Paris: Plon-Nourrit, 1922).
WOOD, NORMA, " Verlaine's vocabulary technique in his later period." M. A. thesis, Ohio State University, 1929.

X

THE PRESENT DAY

97. THE WORLD WAR

The major event of contemporary history is the World War. Because of the number of men involved and the fact that these were enrolled in civilian armies, there was an unprecedented social mixture. The university professor, the denizen of La Villette's stockyard settlements, the boulevardier and the peasant were in the closest of contact over a long period. An elaborate argot developed: It was no longer a question of *souliers, pantalons, café, viande, confortable,* but their corresponding slang equivalents: *grôles, falzars, jus de chapeau, batack, pépère.* Some of it, like *jus,* is today part of the military slang, but, with the exception of a decreasing number of soldier tales, one hears very little of the once rich array of terms embracing every field of the *poilu's* existence. There seems to be a reaction against it, as against all memories of the war.

It is safe to say that present linguistic evolution is being profoundly affected by the advent of new types of communication. The " talkies " and the radio are giving an importance to the oral aspects of language previously unknown and perhaps today unsuspected. The altogether astounding ease with which mechanical appliances are coming into the hands of even the bookish classes means a revolution in the daily life of the layman and tends to bring him into close contact with the life and thought of the chauffeur, the mechanic, the repair man, and others whose superior competence in matters mechanical the layman must often recognize and from whose language we find it difficult to escape. He will shorten *Télégraphie sans Fils* to T.S.F., *méchanicien* to *mécano,* perhaps. Advertising, a world-wide fetish apparently, falls in with the most radical tendencies, be it word-shortening or pseudo-scientific combinations in *–ine* or *–ose* attached to the names of the multiple cures that flood the market. The billboard-syntax and morphology are enough to send shudders down the back of the purist.

98. LITERARY TRENDS

We have seen how the trend of the nineteenth century was, with some notable exceptions, in the direction of greater numbers of oddities and more brilliant eccentricities, more or less designed to *épater le bourgeois*. The poor bourgeois is now become indifferent and allows the most extreme to go their way, paying little attention even to such dicta as these: "*il faut détruire la syntaxe en disposant les substantifs au hasard de leur naissance. Tout ordre étant fatalement un produit de l'intelligence cauteleuse, il faut orchestrer les images en les disposant suivant un maximum de désordre . . .*"[1] The deepening of the gulf between written and spoken language goes on. Yet the tradition to write clearly and with elegance is not gone. Writers like Péguy and Maurras are classic in sympathy; and even in novels where dialect is used, as in the works of Estaunié (1862–   ) or the writings of the "populistes" where vulgar speech might enter, there is the desire to be simple, to avoid the queer and startling. Critics have entered the field against the arch-innovators; witness André Thérive, of whose book *Le français langue morte* we give the main ideas: (1) There is a growing tendency to write French in a manner inconsistent with the genius of the language. (2) This is due, not only to the prevalent literary modes, but also to the influence of foreign concepts, brought in via foreign language habits of polyglot writers. (3) The language of the masses, far from being able to restore naturalness, is itself impregnated with bizarre traits, the immediate product of the music hall, the "talkie," the advertisements, the oddities of journalism and, in general, whatever may be easily copied from the upper strata in the form of set expressions and conversational tinsel. (4) The position of French as a language of culture is threatened, at home and abroad. (5) The remedy is to stop the evolution of the literary language, to conventionalize it to the degree that it will be "dead": "*Tuons-la* (the language), *puisque c'est morte qu'elle peut survivre.*" French will then occupy the position of Latin and Greek (of Attica), both of which survived the political collapse of the states they represented. Much the same point of view had been previously expressed by the conservative Brunetière: "*En tout temps et par tout pays, les langues littéraires ne sont sorties que de l'épuration même et, si l'on veut bien nous passer le mot, de la décantation de la langue populaire.*" Like Thérive, he implied that the popular language was a sediment,

---

[1] Marinetti, *Manifeste technique de la littérature futuriste, cit.* Vossler, p. 378.

a precipitate insoluble in the liquid and from which this liquid, the *pure* language, the literary one, could be poured off without any true reaction having taken place between them. An answer is contained in an article by A. Dubeux (cf. bibliography), bearing the title *Le français langue vivante.* Dubeux challenges principally Thérive's statement that the speech of the masses is radical in its acquisitive processes; he points out that many a barbarism is not a novelty but, on the contrary, is often an archaism. Even argot, however artificial it might be at times, contains many remnants of the fifteenth century. This is a fact easily corroborated. An analysis of military slang during the war showed much patois, eminently conservative therefore. Dauzat[2] points out *maquiller* as hailing from Renaissance argot, while *roupiller*, under a more genteel guise, has been in the language since 1718. As to the " *crise du français* " that Thérive and a host of others have been decrying somewhat vociferously, M. Brunot[3] answers: " *Est-ce à dire que cette ' crise ' nous menace d'une révolution ? Nullement; le français a traversé, au cours des siècles, diverses périodes de troubles graves, où il n'a jamais perdu son caractère. Le génie de la race, fait de sagesse et de goût, l'a tiré des pires aventures.*" Where, according to Brunot, lies the remedy ? With the Academy ? Surely not. The latter has lost its authority and does not satisfy the public's expectancy. It is slow and its dictionary is always behind the times. The new Academy dictionary shows the omission of even officially accepted terms like *aéropostal.* Under these circumstances, it is better to have a consulting *Bureau d'Observations* composed of professional students of linguistics, men of letters, and cultivated laymen or " usagers " who know the language well. Such a body would not attempt to stop the flow of a language nor would its authority be arbitrarily exercised.

The most effective balance is that of French bourgeois conservatism, the affection of that class for the cherished traditions of linguistic elegance and clarity. The enormous sale of the Academy's grammar (1932) and the equally great *succès de librairie* of Brunot's *Observations sur la grammaire de l'Académie* are sufficient assurance that the cultivated classes of France are still linguistically conscious to a degree perhaps unequaled elsewhere. These people are trained in the high standards of the *lycées.* But Brunot believes that the schools are overconservative, that they are enforcing obsolete rules,

[2] *Langue frçse. d'auj.*, p. 20.
[3] *Gr. hist.* Introduction, p. xlvii.

wherein they have been aided, at least indirectly, by the Academy's pronouncements. A few specimens of Brunot's somewhat caustic comments may give his point of view:

Acad. p. 28: Le nom peut être remplacé devant (le) verbe par un pronom, *il* ou *ce*, sujet apparent. Dans les phrases: *C'était un Espagnol de l'armée en déroute. Le temps, c'est de l'argent. Il y eut un fort orage. Il tombait une neige épaisse.* . . .

Observ. p. 33: Adoptons ce procédé d'analyse logique, qui nous ramène à cent cinquante ans en arrière. . . .

Acad. p. 1: La grammaire, que l'on définit " l'art de parler et d'écrire correctement . . . "

Brunot, id.: Qui, " on "? L'Académie accepte-t-elle cette définition archaïque? Elle n'ose pas le dire, et en même temps elle ne veut donner à la grammaire son caractère véritable.

Brunot, p. 17 (Obs.): L'Académie fait assez bon marché de l'orthographe dont elle est le rempart. Elle y reconnaît même des anomalies " Qu'on ne saurait ni expliquer ni encore moins justifier." (p. 9). Précieux aveu! Cependant le Dictionnaire nouveau conserve pieusement les " anomalies " injustifiables. L'usage le veut, n'est-ce pas? L'Académie n'en est plus à 1740, où elle a corrigé des milliers de mots. Elle avait alors des grammairiens. Saluons la mémoire de l'abbé d'Olivet!

99. THE " TOLÉRANCES "

The burden of simplifying the prescriptions of usage was considered in 1899 by the ministry of Public Instruction under the leadership of Georges Leygues. The result was a list of *Tolérances*, i.e., departures from prescribed syntax or spelling " tolerated " in examinations for government functions. It was announced that certain features would no longer be insisted upon in primary or secondary instruction. We have reproduced this list as Appendix II of our book.

There was some dissatisfaction aroused. Brunetière, of classic sympathies and conservative in linguistics, politics, and literature, ridiculed *fous amours* in the plural, permitted instead of the archaic but current *folles amours;* he also scoffed at the tolerated omission of the hyphen and the sympathy exhibited by the Ministry toward simplified orthography. His tactics in this respect consist of taking a few verses of some great poet and dressing them up in as queer an orthographic garb as he can.[4]

Some of the reforms were obeyed, many were hidden under a

[4] Cf. *Rev. deux mondes*, Sept. 1, 1900, p. 148.

cloak of indifference. At any rate, the opposition was not too active. The campaign for spelling reform has a different history. Begun auspiciously under favor of M. Briand, Minister of Public Instruction, with the appointment of Paul Meyer and Antoine Thomas, eminent philologists, along with others less celebrated, to a committee for handling the question, spelling reform ended with an " elegant burial," thanks to many factors: (1) The opposition of the Academy, that august company having been treated by the ministerial committee of 1900 with aloofness. (2) Lack of uniformity in the various systems proposed. (3) Similar lack of system in the conduct of the campaign. (4) Failure to consider the printing industry and other legitimate vested interests. (4) Opposition deriving from the mandarinism of the " *gens de lettres,* jealous of their culture but at the same time possessing a valid argument in the æsthetic character of the visual word with its train of associations.

The reformers have even tried to change the spelling of proper names, with even less success. The present writer has, however, noticed alterations in time tables, such as *Alès* (*Alais,* Gard) and the port of *Sète,* (quondam *Cette*).

It is of no small significance that the leaders in these reform movements were and still are the linguists. We have mentioned Paul Meyer. There are also Thomas (recently deceased), Bréal, and the late dean of the *Faculté des Lettres* at the Sorbonne, F. Brunot. The stand taken by these men is easily accounted for: any self-respecting student of etymology knows that the *g* of *doigt* is an unwarranted restoration after its disappearance back in Gallo-Roman times, also that *poids* is founded on a false derivation (*pondus* instead of the logical *pensum*), propounded during a period when scientific processes had not been discovered and Ménage had nothing to utilize except a very keen intuition. It seems that the orthographic question has fallen to the lot of the *instituteurs,* the elementary teachers, who, tiring of the eternal *dictée* to the exclusion of more important material, have now become the liberals in spelling change. The historians of the French language seem to fear that their program may suffer the same defeat as did that of Meigret. We may note that the otherwise conservative *Revue des deux mondes* has continued certain modifications: *enfans* for *enfants* and other such treatments of final consonants in the plural; the *Revue de philologie française* is more radical.

100. THE "FÉLIBRIGE"

The source of all the movements we have described in this chapter, has been Paris. Evidences of increasing centralization greet us on every hand. There have been reactions, among the noteworthy being the Félibrige, a somewhat mystic name for a group of exceedingly varied membership, whose object is to bring back some of the prestige of Provence and the literary glory that was once associated with the troubadours. Mistral's *Mireille* (1859), based on southern themes, was a world success. In France it was a sensation and was set to music by Gounod on a series of Provençal folk melodies. Mistral (1830–1914) used an artificial *koiné* based on the dialect of Saint-Remy and neighboring towns of the Rhône district. His use of dialect was followed by Aubanel, Roumanille, and by a horde of *félibres* or devotees of the southern Renaissance. It would seem, in recent years, as if the social and political pressure of the capital is too strong. A feeling of inferiority appears to attach still to the dialect, and the regionalistic movement is weakening. Yet a casual visit to Languedoc or Provence will convince anybody that the patois are far from dead. We may also mention local movements in Lille and in the Walloon districts of Belgium, among others. In general, however, ease of communication makes the persistence of a dialect rather difficult.

101. DIALECTS OTHER THAN PROVENÇAL

There are still several foreign tongues spoken in large units on the soil of France. Adjoining the Gascon, a Romance dialect, we have Basque, a non-Indo-European language that once occupied a large part of the Roman province of Aquitaine but which is now retreating steadily, occupying in France only two small districts around the towns of Bayonne and Mauléon. (The Basques of Spain are more numerous and spread over a larger area.) In the same manner, the German dialect, Flemish, is retreating in the north before French. In the peninsula of Brittany, it is true that the Celtic is losing; nevertheless occasional autonomist uprisings, however sporadic and ineffectual, are evidence that regional feeling and the possibilities of a neo-Celtic movement are not entirely dead. What has happened since the war the present writer is in no position to affirm, but in 1918, one could encounter, in the "hinterland" of Saint-Nazaire, more than one old peasant woman, who, asked in French whether she had any vegetables to sell, would barely be able to stammer: " *Attendez, ma fille vient,*" the daughter then carrying on the transaction. The usual villa names are, in Saint-Nazaire proper, prefixed with *Ker* (e.g., *Ker-Gabrielle*), the Celtic word for house.

102. BELGIUM

Linguistic and political boundaries do not, of course, coincide, in most cases. Belgium, situated between Holland and France, finds itself about equally divided, territorially, between French (including the Walloon dialect) and Flemish, closely allied to Dutch. In 1830, when the state was founded, the oligarchy was exclusively French and looked down upon the apparently backward Germanic element. After years of incessant political bickering, still not finished, a kind of linguistic parity has been established between the two parties, the " Flamingants " and the " Fransquillons." The laws of 1932 set up an elaborate machinery for the tactful handling of irritated sensibilities in the public services, the teaching profession and a host of other domains. In the universities, French has perceptibly receded. At Brussels, many courses are in Flemish and the instruction in the University of Ghent is virtually in that language; the exceptions are courses in French literature and allied fields and many offerings in civil engineering for the benefit of the large foreign clientele, disinterested in local linguistic aspirations and more acquainted with French.

Necessarily there have been compromises. Many a Walloon, desirous of entering government service or expanding his business, has learned Flemish. Many an ardent " Flamingant " who works in France or operates, for instance, a hotel in Ostend for a cosmopolitan clientele, must make large concessions to bilingualism.

103. SWITZERLAND

German, French, and Italian have for many years been official; Roumaunsch, spoken in the Alpine valleys of the eastern part, has recently been declared likewise a legal medium.[5] Very roughly speaking, the percentages, in the order mentioned for these languages, are about 70, 20, and 9 respectively, with a bare 1 per cent for the newest linguistic member of the confederation. The can-

---

[5] Cf. *New York Times*, Feb. 26, 1938.

tonal government decides what is the prevailing tongue within its bailiwick, but the greatest latitude is allowed and there is a complete absence of the quarrels that characterize the Belgian situation. The sentiments of the Swiss are admirably expressed in the macaronic couplet reported by Schoell (p. 84), found on a Bernese " brasserie ":

> Ob deutsch ob welsch, c'est tout égal,
> Le même soleil scheint überall.[6]

Romance-speaking Switzerland, known as " la Suisse romande," is specifically the group of cantons called Genève, Vaud, Neuchâtel. The one Italian canton is the Tessino, in the south.

104. ALSACE-LORRAINE

In Alsace-Lorraine, a rigorous analysis is complicated by political considerations. A good deal of Lorraine is solidly French. In Metz one occasionally hears a Germanic patois, but the predominant speech appears to be French. Alsace is Germanic and, with the exception of German immigrants after 1871, speaks an Alemannic dialect, though in the large cities, like Strasbourg, a large part of the population is bilingual. In that city, in 1930, the present writer found no difficulty whatever in making himself understood in French, and in business places he was answered volubly in that tongue. One incident, however, is striking: On asking directions of a family, he was answered by a child of about ten, in German. The mother remonstrated with the child, saying sharply: " *Sprich doch französisch!* " [7] More recent figures show, out of 1,885,823 who answered the questionnaire, 996,568 replied that they knew French, 1,525,043 knew German, 731,029 knew no French and 202,554, no German. In comparison with the German inquiry of 1910, it is revealed that the number of those knowing French has doubled, without, however, any diminution in the German-speaking element. It simply means that bilingualism is on the increase.[8]

---

[6] Be it German or French, it's all the same,
The same sun shines everywhere.

[7] This is but an anecdote; for a thorough and scientific survey, see Levy, *Hist. ling. d'Alsace et de Lorraine* (Paris, 1929).

[8] Bergner, *loc. cit.*

105. CANADA

The continued increase of French is due to several causes: (1) The birth rate among the French Canadians is high, the population having doubled, since 1763, about every forty years, until now it has reached 2,927,000 out of a total of 10,376,786. (2) The church has from early times identified itself with the aspirations of the masses, has taken a leading role in their lives, even to supervising certain material phases of the territorial expansion, so that religion and language are closely interrelated in the minds of these people. An attack on the language is as keenly resented as an attempt against freedom of worship. In the parochial schools French is dominant; religious orders are in constant contact with the former mother country. Where, as in some French-Canadian settlements in the United States, the church has not followed the policy of complete linguistic identification with the people, there has been trouble. (3) The isolation of the French *habitant* on the remote farm or lumber camp. Perhaps all these factors contributed to a family solidarity so great that many a Fraser or MacDougal marrying into a *milieu* not speaking English is often submerged and his children have little interest in the paternal tongue.

It is not easy to generalize as to the character of the French spoken in Canada. There is a class of educated people whose contact with France is sufficient to counteract to a large degree any subversive influences. However, in the main, the purity of a speech not under constant Continental influence and at the same time handled by large numbers of people in contact with English is bound to be impaired. Railroad signs, parallel as they so often are with English, have often something indefinably queer about their style. In advertising, it is not easy to inject the proper Gallic flavor into the legend on some typically American billboard that chants the praises of a school-girl complexion. Canadian newspaper French frequently contains oddities. Press dispatches, received in English and hurriedly translated, bear the unmistakable marks of the original. It is not easy, on the sports pages of Montreal papers, to render an International League game in the language of Bossuet. In the technical realm, up to very recently under English control, that language contains the elements of extensive penetration into the lives of the French-speaking workman, who has been known on occasion to come out with: " *Si vous voulez me spérer un wrench pour settler le washer du sink qui s'est démanché ?* " [9]

[9] Can you spare me a wrench to settle the washer of the sink which is out of order?" Cf. Schoell, p. 127.

A contemporary Probus, M. Etienne Blanchard, has listed the following anglicisms, with corrections, under the caption " Parlons mieux " [10]:

Plutôt que	*Disons*
Elle va graduer cette année	Elle sera diplomée
Set à thé	Service à thé
Stand à musique	Kiosque
Pipe	Calorifère, radiateur
Screen	Paravent

As one goes deeper into the interior of Quebec province, the anglicisms become fewer: *Station de feu > station de pompiers > pompiers.* In the speech of the people one detects the archaisms from the time of the Roi-Soleil and the dialectal traits of the western French patois spoken by the original settlers.

In this province, French is supreme. It has legal parity with English in Ontario, although such cities as Toronto seem to the casual observer devoid of French influence. It is in the vicinity of Ottawa that the problem of parity first became acute.

Socially and culturally the " Canadien " is rising. The rights of his language in political life are no longer seriously challenged. Educational facilities are on the increase.

106. LOUISIANA

In Louisiana French is definitely on the wane. In New Orleans, the failure to revive the French *Opéra* after the fire of 1919 and the cessation of the one French language paper, *L'Abeille*, in 1923, are unmistakable symptoms of the fact. M. Auguste Viatte, writing in 1935, paints the following picture:

Que m'offrira la Nouvelle-Orléans? Je l'ai vue, il y a sept ans; les journaux, les magasins, étaient anglais, mais le patron de mon hôtel téléphonait en français à sa famille, et l'on rencontrait par les rues d'étonnantes vieilles, aux châles bariolés, qui s'abordaient par des: Bonjour, Madame, avec l'accent du Conservatoire... Elles étaient si cassées, si décrépites, qu'enfin elles ont disparu; à peine un ou deux fichus glissent-ils, çà et là; les énormes négresses, entortillées dans leurs foulards, qui surveillent leurs mioches au seuil de la porte, leur criaillent leurs remontrances en mauvais américain....

[10] *Bulletin de la société du parler français au Canada* XV, 1917, 472.

Schoell [11] believes that the moment is not far off when all that will remain to show that New Orleans was a *ville de chez nous* will be its name, those of some of its inhabitants, the Cathédrale Saint-Louis, a few old street signs, and the tombs of the old cemetery.

In the back country, the vitality of French is much greater, notably in the parishes of Saint-Landry, Saint-Martin, Acadia, Beauregard, Evangeline, Pointe-Coupée, Saint-Jean-Baptiste, Lafourche, Terrebonne. Especially the Acadians, descendants of those exiled from Canada in the days of Evangeline, have conserved their language to a much greater degree. The ecclesiastical authorities, notably, have been more favorable than in the city of New Orleans and there is a bishop who knows French as his parish priests and their charges know it.

The characteristics of Louisiana " Creole " French, especially that of the Acadians, resemble the language of their Canadian cousins in the archaic vocabulary and in the dialectal elements (Norman especially). Allowance must be made, as Schoell indicates, for the difference in the flora and fauna of this section of the country as compared to Canada.

There exists a Negro-French, called Gumbo, resembling that of the less cultivated speech of Haiti. This dialect, if such it may be called, is menaced by the inroads of English, especially in this day of easier communications and decreasing isolation.

107. CHANNEL ISLANDS

The situation differs considerably in the various islands of the channel group. In Guernsey, the English influence is very strong, especially in the capital, Saint-Pierre. At least, so it seems to the casual observer. The present writer was told that the British schoolteacher wages active war against the dialect. Schoell alludes to the influx of Englishmen desirous of dodging the income tax [12], in view of the local exemptions; the present writer has noted a predilection for the islands as a vacation resort, even in the case of less wealthy individuals. These circumstances militate to a considerable degree against the survival of French. On the other side of the balance may be cited the following: even in the capital, Norman is the language one hears most about the docks and in the market, on the days, especially when the country folk come in

[11] *Op. cit.*, p. 150.
[12] *Ibid.*, p. 107.

with their produce. There are old families on the island whose primary language is French.

In Jersey, English is less strong: The signs that one sees in the stations of the narrow-gauge road are in both languages, and the same holds for the banks. Schoell mentions a newspaper, the *Chroniques de Jersey*, which has also a comic column in patois. [13]

On the island of Sark, small as it is and more isolated, both semi-feudal institutions and the old dialect are strong. More interesting to the outsider is the retention of French as the language of legal documents, this since about 1530, curiously coinciding with the approximate date of Villers-Cotterets (cf. § 40). The present writer had access to court records of Guernsey, from which a specimen is here quoted:

Le sept Juin mil

neuf centvingt devant Monsieur le Baillif, le Révérend T———— D————, Maître ès Arts, Vicaire de l'Eglise appelée 'Saint James' Church' en la paroisse de Saint Pierre Port, en cette Ile de Guernesey, a déclaré avoir ce matin vers huit heures cinquante ou environ interjeté en présence du Major G———— D———— W———— et de Monsieur A———— G———— une Clameur de Haro aux ouvriers des Etats de cette Ile, lesquels dits ouvriers enlevaient les pierres du trottoir du côté gauche de la rue appelée 'Saint James' Street' le tout au grand préjudice et contre le droit de propriété du dit T———— D———— au dit nom.

Guernesey, ce sept Juin 1920
(signé) Edw. C. Ozanne Baillif

Reçu à 2–55 p.m.
Ce 7 Juin 1920
(signé) A. J. Roussel
Dté. Greffier du Roi

It is interesting to note that the usage of Clameur de Haro is itself very old, most likely from medieval times.

108. COLONIES AND MANDATES

We saw, in the last chapter, how France was beginning to re-acquire a colonial empire. The war added to this territory such areas as parts of West Africa and mandated areas like Syria. Agencies devoted to the propagation of the national language have been at work, religious and lay. Schools and *lycées* have been created by private as well as public initiative.

[13] *Ibid.*, p. 106.

109. SPREAD OF FRENCH

It is not, however, in terms of area units or even in terms of the diplomatic prestige that we should estimate the present importance of French. The fact is that there never was a time when French was more actively studied all over the world than now, for scholars are constantly in touch with one another. One need not speak of the position of French in the American curriculum or American contributions to its scholarly study. The government and private agencies that we have alluded to help to maintain interest. We may mention the Alliance Française, whose chapters exist in all larger American cities and those abroad, and whose lecturers travel far and wide — to say nothing of the summer schools conducted for foreigners in many French universities. Other agencies are the Mission Laïque and the Alliance Universelle Israélite; these are both educational enterprises. The government also sponsors institutes of French culture in a number of cities in Europe and elsewhere.

It is too early as yet to point out definite changes, much less definite trends in the language structure. In the literary styles there is little uniformity. It is perhaps fair to say that syntactic shortening and general economy of connectives has been sought by many — *Un visage gendarme, un succès bœuf* — wherein the noun functions as adjective. We can also observe certain traits being accentuated, traits already under way in the nineteenth century, such as the dying of the imperfect subjunctive and the serious attempts on the life of the subjunctive in general. Some writers enjoy making an intransitive verb transitive, e.g., *vivre une pensée*.[14] The popular language (cf. Bauche) is exercising influence in some instances.[15]

[REFERENCES

BAUCHE, H., *Le langage populaire* (Paris: Payot, 1920).
BEAULIEUX, CH., *Histoire de l'orthographe française.* (Paris: Champion, 1927).
Bulletin de la société du parler français au Canada (Quebec, 1902–).
BRUNETIÈRE, F., " La déformation du français par l'argot," in *Rev. des deux mondes.* Oct. 15, 1881, p. 934; Sept. 1, 1900, p. 148.
DAUZAT, A., *La langue française d'aujourd'hui* (Paris: A. Colin, 1908).

[14] Vossler, p. 380.
[15] Cf. G. Rohlfs, *Volkssprachliche Einflüsse im modernen Französisch* (Berlin, 1928.)

———, *La langue française: sa vie, son évolution* (Paris: Stock, 1926).

———, *Histoire de la langue française* (Paris: Payot, 1930).

De VREESE, M., " De Woorden Flamingant en Franskiljon, *Tijdschrift v. nederlandsche Taal en Letterkunde*, LI (1932), p. 65.

DUBEUX, A., " Le français, langue vivante," *Revue des cours et conférences*, XXV, 571.

DUMAS, G., "La langue française en extrême-Orient," *Rev. des deux mondes*, Mar. 15, 1931, pp. 289.

ESNAULT, G., *Le poilu tel qu'il se parle* (Paris: Rossard, 1919).

GLASER, K., *Neologismus u. Sprachgefühl im heutigen französischen* (Romanisches Seminar., Giessen, 1930).

LERCH, EUG., " Die französische Sprache des 19ten u. 20sten Jahrhunderts," *Neuphil. Mitteilungen*, I (1930), 99–111; 145–58.

LEVY, PAUL, *Histoire linguistique d'Alsace et de Lorraine* (Paris, Soc. d'éd.: " Les Belles Lettres," 1929).

MAURRAS, C., *Théodore Aubanel* (1st ed., Paris: Savine, 1890; Champion, 1928).

MOUFFLET, A., *Encore le massacre de la langue française* (Paris: Didier, 1935).

PREIN, A., *Syntaktisches aus franz. Soldatenbriefen* (Giessener Beiträge Giessen: Selbstverlag des Romanischen Seminars, 1921).

REIDER, G., *Probleme des Kriegsfranzösischen*. Becker Festschrift (Heidelberg, Carl Winter, 1922).

RICHTER, ELISE, " Studien über das neueste Französisch," in *Archiv. f.d. Stud. d. neuer. Sprach. u. Lit.* vol. 135–6 (1916–18).

RIPERT, E., *Le Félibrige* (Paris: A. Colin, 1924).

SCHOELL, FR., *La langue française dans le monde* (Paris: Bibliothèque du " Français Moderne," 1936).

THÉRIVE, A., *Le français, langue morte?* (6th ed., Paris: Plon-Nourrit, 1923; 1930).

APPENDIX I

VAUGELAS: REMARQUES SUR LA LANGUE FRANÇOISE

(1647)

A Classified Table of Contents of the 1647 Edition, with Additional Reference to the Two-Volume Edition of Chassang (1880).

(Note: Numbers in parenthesis refer to the correct page number of pages numbered incorrectly; after page 256 there is an omission to page 297, and after page 491 there follows page 452; no corrections have been made in these places.)

I. LEXICOGRAPHY

B. Semantics

C. GENDER

D. Spelling Variants

E. ARCHAISMS

F. OTHER INCORRECT FORMS AND WORDS

G. Correct Forms and Words

II. SYNTAX

A. Nouns

C. Adjectives

D. VERBS

E. ADVERBS

III. STYLE

A. CLARITY

B. EUPHONY

C. Form

D. Word Order

APPENDIX II

Rapport et Arrêté relatifs à la simplification de l'enseignement de la Syntaxe française.

31 Juillet 1900.

1° Rapport présenté au nom de la Commission chargée de préparer la simplification de l'enseignement de la syntaxe française dans les Écoles primaires et secondaires (M. P. Clairin, rapporteur).

Messieurs, conformément à l'article 7 du décret du 11 mars 1898, M. le Ministre de l'Instruction publique demanda, le 10 janvier 1900, l'avis du Conseil supérieur sur le vœu déposé par MM. Clairin et Bernès, tendant à la nomination d'une Commission chargée de préparer la simplification de la syntaxe française enseignée dans les Écoles primaires et secondaires.

Suivant le règlement, la Section permanente avait, au préalable, étudié ce vœu, l'avait accueilli favorablement et avait émis l'avis de renvoyer la proposition, pour examen, au Conseil supérieur en séance plénière.

Cette proposition fut adoptée conformément à l'article 5 de la loi du 27 février 1880, qui attribue au Conseil supérieur le droit de donner son avis sur les programmes, méthodes d'enseignement et modes d'examen déjà étudiés par la Section permanente.

Un arrêté de M. le Ministre de l'Instruction publique en date du 13 janvier 1900 composa la Commission des membres suivants du Conseil supérieur: MM. Gaston Paris, *Président*, Gréard, Croiset, Paul Meyer, Bernès, Clairin, Devinat, Comte. Le 20 janvier, la Commission tenait sa première séance et entreprenait le travail dont on l'avait chargée. C'est le résultat de ce travail que le présent rapport est destiné à vous faire connaître et pour lequel la Commission demande un nouvel avis favorable du Conseil supérieur.

La Commission n'avait pas qualité pour légiférer en matière de langage; elle s'est abstenue, avec le plus grand soin, d'édicter aucune règle nouvelle; elle ne prétend obliger personne à se conformer à ses propositions ni même à en prendre connaissance, excepté cependant les maîtres chargés d'enseigner la grammaire, car ceux-ci doivent se tenir au courant de tous les travaux qui peuvent leur permettre de simplifier et d'améliorer leur enseignement. On peut être certain qu'ils ne négligeront pas de le faire. Nous en avons la preuve par ce qui s'est déjà passé dans l'enseignement secondaire, où les professeurs ont profité des travaux publiés tant en France qu'à l'étranger pour apprendre à leurs élèves les formes grecques vraiment classiques au lieu des formes de la langue commune ou de divers dialectes qu'on apprenait encore il y a peu d'années. Les membres des Commissions d'examen auront aussi à tenir compte des propositions qui vous sont soumises, *car c'est une tolérance large et intelligente dans les examens qui est le véritable objet de la réforme proposée.*

Dans le travail de simplification qu'elle était chargée d'entreprendre, la Commission a jugé qu'elle ne devait rien autoriser qui pût porter atteinte à la bonne tradition de la langue. Certaines complications apparentes, certaines exceptions aux règles générales constituent des idiotismes qu'on ne saurait supprimer sans inconvénient. La présence de deux membres éminents de l'Académie française, dont l'un présidait la Commission; celle du doyen de la Faculté des Lettres de l'Université de Paris, non moins délicat lettré que savant helléniste, sont une garantie que nul attentat n'a été commis contre la langue littéraire; la présence des maîtres les plus connus de l'enseignement historique des langues romanes assure aussi le travail de la Commission contre toute hérésie historique et grammaticale. Presque toujours les décisions ont été prises à l'unanimité, quelquefois seulement à une forte majorité, et les procès-verbaux témoignent que les séances ont été suivies avec une assiduité exemplaire.

La Commission n'a pas oublié non plus que tous les grammairiens français ne méritent pas le mal qui a été dit des grammairiens en général, que ceux du xviiie siècle en particulier ont fait souvent des choses excellentes. Leurs travaux minutieux sur la syntaxe ont contribué à améliorer la langue française. Grâce à eux, la clarté, qualité dominante de notre langue, a toujours été en grandissant. On commettrait une faute si on laissait la langue écrite revenir à la confusion d'où elle est sortie à son avantage.

Mais, à côté des grammairiens auxquels le français est redevable d'une partie de ses qualités, il en a existé d'autres, de beaucoup inférieurs, auxquels on doit une partie de la grammaire actuelle, des règles compliquées, subtiles et inutiles, rendant quelquefois impossible la construction des phrases les plus simples. Malgré l'autorité des meilleurs écrivains, qui ont ignoré ou refusé d'appliquer un très grand nombre de ces règles, on exige qu'elles soient connues et appliquées par les élèves des classes primaires, par les candidats à tous les examens. Quand on lit les grammaires françaises élémentaires, et surtout les exercices qui y sont joints, on est étonné du nombre considérable de complications et de subtilités qu'on y trouve. Les règles, simples en apparence, donnent naissance à une foule de remarques qui deviennent autant de sujets d'exercices, c'est-à-dire de problèmes. Plus on invente de ces problèmes, surtout s'ils sont bien compliqués, plus on montre la finesse de son esprit. On en arrive à se complaire dans la science des exceptions réelles ou simplement possibles.

L'enseignement élémentaire perd le caractère de simplicité, qui devrait toujours être le sien, pour se hérisser de subtilités. Avec cette préoccupation de raffiner, les choses les plus simples en apparence cachent des pièges.

Ainsi, dans une phrase telle que celle-ci: *ils ont ôté leur(s) chapeau(x)*, devra-t-on écrire *chapeau(x)* au singulier ou au pluriel ? Au singulier, disent les uns, puisque chaque personne n'a qu'un chapeau; au pluriel, disent les autres, puisqu'il y a plusieurs personnes et par conséquent plusieurs chapeaux. Autre exemple: « Il faut écrire *groseille* au singulier dans l'expression *du sirop de groseille*, parce que, réduites en sirop, les groseilles ont perdu leur forme; mais il faut écrire *groseilles* au pluriel dans l'expression *des confitures de groseilles de Bar*, parce que dans ces confitures les groseilles restent entières. » N'est-il pas regrettable que des Commissions d'examen, qui doivent être composées de personnes intelligentes, s'arrêtent à discuter de semblables puérilités, au lieu d'accepter indifféremment le singulier ou le pluriel, sans se soucier de l'orthographe du texte imprimé qu'elles ont sous les yeux ? Que penser d'une explication comme la suivante: « Il faut dire: les arbres les plus hauts sont *les plus exposés* à la tempête, parce que le rapport du superlatif est déterminé, mais on a abattu les arbres *le plus exposés* à la tempête, parce que le rapport n'est pas déterminé ? » Est-ce là ce qu'il convient d'enseigner à des enfants; et, s'ils parviennent à apprendre par cœur des règles semblables, quel profit en retire leur intelligence ?

Après avoir constaté ce vice qui existe à des degrés différents dans toutes les grammaires, la Commission s'est décidée à rechercher, pour les supprimer, les règles subtiles, parfois fausses, qui encombrent l'enseignement élémentaire et qui ne servent à rien ni pour la lecture des textes, ni pour la formation de l'esprit et le développement de la réflexion.

Les grammaires et les exercices contiennent aussi bien des choses simplement inutiles, qui sont à leur place dans les dictionnaires, mais dont on ne doit pas s'embarrasser dans l'enseignement élémentaire. Ainsi, par exemple, le pluriel irrégulier des mots *ciel, œil, travail*, etc., ainsi la différence de signification, suivant le genre masculin ou féminin, des mots tels que *œuvre, période, relâche*, etc. La grammaire n'a pas à enseigner les formes et les significations spéciales que certains mots ont prises dans les langues techniques. C'est seulement à ceux qui étudieront les différents métiers, ou à ceux qui veulent faire une étude universelle de la langue, qu'il appartient d'apprendre de pareils détails. A quoi bon se préoccuper de la manière d'écrire au pluriel *fête-Dieu, bain-marie*, quand on ne peut trouver aucun exemple du pluriel de ces mots, à moins d'inventer des constructions hors de l'usage habituel ? A quoi servent tant d'exercices obscurs sur les homonymes, les paronymes, véritable casse-tête toujours en honneur, qu'on trouve jusque dans les devoirs choisis pour figurer à l'Exposition de 1900 ?

En retranchant tant de choses inutiles qui ne sont pas du domaine grammatical, et qui compliquent sans profit l'enseignement élémentaire du français, la Commission a été amenée tout naturellement à fixer, en quelque manière, les bases de cet enseignement en déterminant ce qu'il est bon de garder dans les livres élémentaires et ce qu'il faudrait en éliminer. Elle a jugé que, dans l'enseignement élémentaire, on devrait se borner aux règles générales; que les subtilités grammaticales n'étaient pas là à leur place; que les constructions particulières, rares, exceptionnelles devaient être notées, étudiées dans la lecture et l'explication des textes, avec des élèves plus avancés dans la connaissance du français.

On trouve encore dans les grammaires élémentaires trop de règles compliquées que les enfants sont réduits à apprendre par cœur et à appliquer au hasard, sans essayer de les comprendre, parce que, plus on y réfléchit, moins on les comprend. Ainsi, par exemple, celui qui veut parler correctement, d'après la grammaire, ne doit pas apprendre moins de cinq règles différentes pour être capable de faire accorder en genre l'adjectif avec le mot *gens*. Ainsi encore, c'est par une série interminable de règles compliquées qu'on apprend dans quels cas il faut faire accorder le participe passé et dans quels cas il faut le laisser invariable; et, lorsqu'on croit savoir ces règles, on reste embarrassé dans les exercices où il faudrait les appliquer, tant on y trouve de pièges, si bien qu'il faut se résigner à apprendre et à savoir par cœur d'interminables listes d'exemples dont on cherche à faire une imitation mécanique sans les comprendre. Et si on étudie scientifiquement ces règles si compliquées, on constate qu'elles sont quelquefois contraires à l'évolution naturelle de la langue française. Si même on admet qu'elles peuvent, jusqu'à un certain point, aider à l'analyse de la pensée, les difficultés qu'elles présentent sont hors de proportion avec le service rendu.

Contre cette réglementation exagérée qui ne sert ni à la clarté ni à la pureté de la langue, ni à la formation de l'intelligence, la Commission a cherché à réagir en recommandant dans beaucoup de cas une tolérance éclairée.

Deux exemples suffiront à montrer quelle méthode la Commission a suivie pour arriver à la simplification. L'un est relatif aux noms composés, l'autre à l'accord du participe passé: deux questions particulièrement longues et embrouillées dans toutes les grammaires.

Si on veut écrire aujourd'hui un nom composé, on n'est jamais sûr de le faire correctement, car des mots tout à fait semblables se rencontrent écrits de différentes manières aussi bien dans les publications officielles que dans le Dictionnaire de l'Académie (des *timbres-poste*, mais des *trains-postes* ou des *trains poste*, des *paquebots-poste*), et les dictionnaires se contredisent entre eux. La Commission, tout en autorisant l'usage actuel pour ceux qui le connaissent, ou croient le connaître, a essayé de classer les mots par groupes naturels d'après les éléments qui servent à les constituer; elle autorise la séparation ou la réunion des éléments constitutifs en permettant soit de traiter les noms composés comme des mots simples pour la formation du pluriel, soit d'appliquer les règles générales de la formation du pluriel à chacun des éléments. En permettant de plus et même en conseillant de supprimer dans tous ces mots le trait d'union, qui en réalité ne sert à rien, elle fait disparaître une des causes de fautes les plus fréquentes, car sur ce point encore on ne saurait rien imaginer de plus confus et de moins logique que les règles et l'usage d'aujourd'hui.

Dès qu'on a parlé de simplifier la syntaxe, tous ceux qui ont émis un avis sur la question ont pensé tout d'abord aux règles d'accord du participe passé. Le fait est curieux, et cependant très naturel. C'est que nous avons tous gardé le souvenir de la complication de ces règles, du temps qu'on passe à les apprendre pour se trouver embarrassé dès qu'il faut les appliquer dans des constructions un peu douteuses. La règle générale, logique à l'origine, est, pour ceux qui réfléchissent, une de celles qui doivent disparaître dans le développement naturel du français. Lorsqu'on a cessé de faire accorder dans tous les cas le participe passé avec le complément direct du verbe, de dire, par exemple, *j'ai écrite la lettre*, on s'est engagé dans une voie qui devait conduire à regarder le participe joint à l'auxiliaire comme une forme invariable: *j'ai écrit* est en réalité aujourd'hui un simple temps de verbe, comme *j'écrivais* ou *j'écrivis*. Cette assimilation est tellement naturelle que la règle imposée actuellement comme obligatoire, et si peu observée d'ailleurs dans le langage parlé, n'a jamais été franchement acceptée. Les meilleurs écrivains ne l'ont pas toujours appliquée, même en prose, même lorsque la prononciation permet de distinguer le féminin du masculin. Les grammairiens ont imaginé une foule de raisons pour justifier l'absence d'accord suivant que tel mot précède ou suit le participe, suivant les différents sens des mêmes participes, de sorte que la règle s'est comme entourée et hérissée d'exceptions, de complications qu'on apprend par un effort de mémoire au moment des examens et qu'on oublie aussitôt après. De plus, si la règle d'accord toute simple peut, lorsqu'elle est bien appliquée, indiquer jusqu'à un certain point l'analyse de la pensée, la même règle imposée aux participes des verbes réfléchis est expliquée dans les grammaires d'une manière vraiment monstrueuse, contraire à la vérité et à la logique. En permettant de laisser toujours invariable le participe passé joint à l'auxiliaire *avoir*, ainsi que dans les verbes réfléchis, la Commission permet de supprimer dans les grammaires élémentaires tout un chapitre des plus fatigants, des plus inutiles, un de ceux qui contribuent le plus à rebuter les étrangers.

La Commission ne prétend nullement restreindre l'étude du français. Les maîtres qui s'adressent à un auditoire assez avancé, tel que celui des classes supérieures de l'enseignement secondaire ou de l'enseignement primaire, à plus forte raison les maîtres de l'enseignement supérieur sont et resteront libres de donner à l'étude du français toute l'étendue qu'ils jugeront nécessaire, de relever, de signaler toutes les finesses du langage; et, dans leurs compositions, les élèves et les étudiants pourront librement montrer toute leur science grammaticale et littéraire.

La Commission n'a pas dépassé les limites que vous aviez assignées à son travail. Elle se contente d'indiquer jusqu'où peut et doit aller dans les examens la tolérance en matière de syntaxe française. Elle croit qu'on arrivera ainsi, sans nuire à notre langue nationale, à débarrasser l'enseignement d'une foule de subtilités et de difficultés qui le compliquent sans aucun profit.

Elle vous propose donc d'émettre l'avis que, dans tous les examens qui comportent une épreuve d'orthographe directe ou indirecte, les simplifications dont la liste est donnée à la suite de ce rapport seront tolérées et qu'on n'aura pas le droit de compter de fautes aux candidats qui useront de la liberté ainsi accordée.

Convaincue de n'avoir rien admis qui puisse porter atteinte à la langue française, la Commission est d'avis qu'il sera bon de tolérer même dans les examens qui ne comportent pas une véritable épreuve d'orthographe, tels que le baccalauréat, tout ce qu'on aura décidé de tolérer dans les examens où existe une épreuve d'orthographe.

Les complications, les subtilités inutiles chassées des examens, et par suite des exercices préparatoires aux examens, disparaîtront de l'enseignement élémentaire. On ne manquera pas de préférer le simple au compliqué, le facile au difficile, dès que la connaissance du compliqué et du difficile ne sera plus d'aucune utilité. Mais nul maître ne sera gêné, nul auteur de grammaire ne se trouvera particulièrement atteint. Les maîtres pourront seulement simplifier leur enseignement en en supprimant la partie la plus ingrate; les auteurs et les éditeurs pourront diminuer l'épaisseur de leurs livres en supprimant bon nombre de pages. Nulle addition, beaucoup de suppressions, tel est le résultat auquel arrive la Commission.

Le bénéfice de la réforme existera tout d'abord pour les enfants, dont le travail deviendra moins fastidieux et plus intelligent. Au lieu de charger leur mémoire de règles inutiles qu'ils se hâtent d'oublier, ils pourront lire et expliquer beaucoup plus de textes français. En outre, à une époque où la diffusion du français est rendue de plus en plus difficile, on peut espérer qu'une grammaire plus courte, plus claire, plus simple, contribuera à augmenter le nombre de ceux qui apprendront notre langue. Les étrangers qui viennent chaque année faire dans notre pays une étude du français à la fois savante et pratique accueilleront certainement avec plaisir la simplification préparée par la Commission.

Il sera bon que les administrations qui ne dépendent pas de l'Instruction publique s'entendent pour admettre dans leurs examens particuliers la même tolérance que la Commission vous propose d'autoriser dans les examens de l'enseignement primaire et de l'enseignement secondaire. Il ne faudrait pas que les élèves des Écoles publiques eussent à souffrir d'un manque de concordance entre les règlements des différentes administrations.

Signé: P. CLAIRIN.

2° Arrêté [1]

Le Ministre de l'Instruction publique et des Beaux-Arts,
Vu l'article 5 de la loi du 27 février 1880;
Le Conseil supérieur de l'Instruction publique entendu,
Arrête:

[1] Voir la *Note présentée à la Commission du Dictionnaire de l'Académie française* par M. GRÉARD; in-8° de 32 pages (Paris, Colin, 1893).

ARTICLE 1ᵉʳ. — Dans les examens ou concours dépendant du Ministère de l'Instruction publique qui comportent des épreuves spéciales d'orthographe, il ne sera pas compté de fautes aux candidats pour avoir usé des tolérances indiquées dans la liste annexée au présent arrêté.

La même disposition est applicable au jugement des diverses compositions rédigées en langue française, dans les examens ou concours dépendant du Ministère de l'Instruction publique qui ne comportent pas une épreuve spéciale d'orthographe.

ART. 2. — Dans les établissements d'enseignement public de tout ordre, les usages et prescriptions contraires aux indications énoncées dans la liste annexée au présent arrêté ne seront pas enseignés comme règles.

Liste annexée à l'Arrêté du 31 juillet 1900

SUBSTANTIF

Nombre des substantifs. — Témoin. — Placé en tête d'une proposition, ce mot pourra rester invariable ou prendre la marque du pluriel, si le substantif qui le suit est au pluriel. Ex.: *témoin* ou *témoins les victoires qu'il a remportées.* La même liberté sera accordée pour le mot *témoin* dans la locution *prendre à témoin.* Ex.: *je vous prends tous à témoin* ou *à témoins.*

Pluriel ou singulier. — Dans toutes les constructions où le sens permet de comprendre le substantif complément aussi bien au singulier qu'au pluriel, on tolérera l'emploi de l'un ou l'autre nombre. Ex.: *des habits de femme* ou *de femmes; — des confitures de groseille* ou *de groseilles; — des prêtres en bonnet carré* ou *en bonnets carrés; — ils ont ôté leur chapeau* ou *leurs chapeaux.*

SUBSTANTIFS DES DEUX GENRES

1. Aigle. — L'usage actuel donne à ce substantif le genre masculin. Les auteurs les plus classiques l'ont aussi employé au féminin. On tolérera le féminin comme le masculin. Ex.: *un aigle* ou *une aigle.*

2. Amour, orgue. — L'usage actuel donne à ces deux mots le genre masculin au singulier. Au pluriel, on tolérera indifféremment le genre masculin ou le genre féminin. Ex.: *les grandes orgues; — un des plus beaux orgues.*

3. Délice et délices sont, en réalité, deux mots différents. Le premier est d'un usage rare et un peu recherché. Il est inutile de s'en occuper dans l'enseignement élémentaire et dans les exercices.

4. Automne, enfant. — Ces deux mots étant des deux genres, il est inutile de s'en occuper particulièrement. Il en est de même de tous les substantifs qui sont indifféremment des deux genres.

5. Gens, orge. — On tolérera, dans toutes les constructions, l'accord de l'adjectif au féminin avec le mot *gens*. Ex.: *instruits* ou *instruites par l'expérience, les vieilles gens sont soupçonneux* ou *soupçonneuses*.

On tolérera l'emploi du mot *orge* au féminin sans exception: *orge carrée, orge mondée, orge perlée*.

6. Hymne. — Il n'y a pas de raison suffisante pour donner à ce mot deux sens différents, suivant qu'il est employé au masculin ou au féminin. On tolérera les deux genres, aussi bien pour les chants nationaux que pour les chants religieux. Ex.: *un bel hymne* ou *une belle hymne*.

7. Œuvre. — Si, dans quelques expressions, ce mot est employé au masculin, cet usage est fondé sur une différence de sens bien subtile. On tolérera l'emploi du mot au féminin dans tous les sens. Ex.: *une grande œuvre, la grande œuvre*.

8. Pâques. — On tolérera l'emploi de ce mot au féminin aussi bien pour désigner une date que la fête religieuse. Ex.: *à Pâques prochain* ou *à Pâques prochaines*.

9. Période. — Même au sens spécial où on exige actuellement le genre masculin, on tolérera l'emploi de ce mot au féminin. Ex.: *arriver à la plus haute période* ou *au plus haut période*.

PLURIEL DES SUBSTANTIFS

Pluriel des noms propres. — La plus grande obscurité régnant dans les règles et les exceptions enseignées dans les grammaires, on tolérera dans tous les cas que les noms propres, précédés de l'article pluriel, prennent la marque du pluriel. Ex.: *les Corneilles* comme *les Gracques*, — *des Virgiles* (exemplaires) comme *des Virgiles* (éditions).

Il en sera de même pour les noms propres de personnes désignant les œuvres de ces personnes. Ex.: *des Meissoniers*.

Pluriel des noms empruntés à d'autres langues. — Lorsque ces mots sont tout à fait entrés dans la langue française, on tolérera que le pluriel soit formé suivant la règle générale. Ex.: *des exéats* comme *des déficits*.

NOMS COMPOSÉS

Noms composés. — Les mêmes noms composés se rencontrent aujourd'hui tantôt avec le trait d'union, tantôt sans trait d'union. Il est inutile de fatiguer les enfants à apprendre des contradictions que rien ne justifie. L'absence de trait d'union dans l'expression *pomme de terre* n'empêche pas cette expression de former un véritable mot composé aussi bien que *chef-d'œuvre*, par exemple.

Chacun restera libre de se conformer aux règles actuelles; mais on tolérera la simplification des règles relatives aux noms composés d'après les principes suivants:

1° Noms composés d'un verbe suivi d'un substantif. — On pourra les écrire en un seul mot formant le pluriel d'après la règle générale. Ex.: *un essuiemain, des essuiemains;* — *un abatjour, des abatjours;* — *un fessemathieu, des fessemathieux;* — *un gagnepetit, des gagnepetits;* — *un gardecôte, des gardecôtes.*

Mais on conservera les deux mots séparés dans les expressions comme *garde forestier, garde général,* où la présence de l'adjectif indique clairement que *garde* est un substantif.

2° Noms composés d'un substantif suivi d'un adjectif. — On pourra réunir ou séparer les deux éléments. Les deux mots ou le mot composé formeront le pluriel d'après la règle générale. Ex.: *un coffre fort* ou *coffrefort, des coffres forts* ou *coffreforts.*

3° Noms composés d'un adjectif suivi d'un substantif. — Même liberté. Ex.: *une basse cour* ou *bassecour, des basses cours* ou *bassecours;* — *un blanc seing* ou *blancseing, des blancs seings* ou *blancseings;* — *un blanc bec* ou *blancbec, des blancs becs* ou *blancbecs.*

On exceptera *bonhomme* et *gentilhomme,* mots pour lesquels l'usage a établi un pluriel intérieur sensible à l'oreille: *des bonshommes, des gentilshommes.*

On pourra écrire en un seul mot, sans apostrophe: *grandmère, grandmesse, grandroute.*

4° Noms composés d'un adjectif et d'un substantif désignant un objet nouveau appelé du nom d'une de ses qualités. — Même liberté. Ex.: *un rouge gorge* ou *rougegorge, des rouges gorges* ou *rougegorges.*

5° Noms composés de deux adjectifs désignant une personne ou une chose. — Les deux mots pourront s'écrire séparément, sans trait d'union, chacun gardant sa vie propre. Ex.: *un sourd muet, une sourde muette, des sourds muets, des sourdes muettes;* — *douce amère,* etc.

6° Noms composés de deux substantifs construits en apposition. — On pourra ou écrire les deux mots séparément, chacun formant son pluriel d'après la règle générale, ou les réunir, sans trait d'union, en un seul mot qui ne prendra qu'une fois, à la fin, la marque du pluriel. Ex.: *un chou fleur* ou *choufleur, des choux fleurs* ou *choufleurs;* — *un chef lieu* ou *cheflieu, des chefs lieux* ou *cheflieux.*

7° Noms composés de deux substantifs ou d'un substantif et d'un adjectif dont l'un est en réalité le complément de l'autre, sans particule marquant l'union. — On pourra toujours réunir les deux mots en un seul, prenant à la fin la marque du pluriel d'après la règle générale. Ex.: *un timbreposte, des timbrepostes;* — *un terreplein, des terrepleins.*

Pour les mots *hôtel Dieu, fête Dieu,* il semble préférable de conserver l'usage actuel et de séparer les éléments constitutifs. Cependant on ne comptera pas de faute à ceux qui réuniront les deux substantifs en un seul mot: *hôtel-dieu, fêtedieu.*

Quant au pluriel des mots *hôtel Dieu, fête Dieu, bain marie,* il n'y a pas lieu de s'en occuper, puisque ces mots sont inusités au pluriel. Il est inutile aussi de s'occuper, dans l'enseignement élémentaire et dans les exercices du pluriel, du mot *trou madame,* désignant un jeu inusité aujourd'hui.

8° Noms composés d'un adjectif numéral pluriel et d'un substantif ou d'un adjectif. — On pourra les écrire en un seul mot et laisser au second la marque du pluriel, même au singulier. Ex.: *un troismâts, des troismâts; — un troisquarts, des troisquarts.*

Gréard. *Lég. de l'Instr. primaire,* VI.

9° Noms composés de deux substantifs unis par une particule indiquant le rapport qui existe entre eux. — On écrira séparément les éléments de ces mots en observant avec chacun les règles générales de la syntaxe. Ex.: *un chef d'œuvre, des chefs d'œuvre; — un pot au feu, des pots au feu; — un pied d'alouette, des pieds d'alouette; — un tête à tête, des tête à tête.*

10° Noms composés d'éléments variés empruntés à des substantifs, à des verbes, à des adjectifs, à des adverbes, à des mots étrangers. — On tolérera la séparation ou la réunion des éléments. Si on les réunit en un seul mot, celui-ci pourra former son pluriel comme un mot simple. Ex.: *un chassé croisé* ou *un chassécroisé, des chassés croisés* ou *des chassécroisés; — un fier à bras* ou *un fierabras, des fiers à bras* ou *des fierabras; — un pique nique* ou *un piquenique, des pique niques* ou *des piqueniques; — un soi disant* ou *un soi-disant, des soi disant* ou *des soidisants; — un te Deum* ou *un tedeum, des te Deum* ou *des tedeums; — un ex voto* ou *un exvoto, des ex voto* ou *des exvotos; — un vice roi* ou *un viceroi, des vice rois* ou *des vicerois; — un en tête* ou *un entête, des en têtes* ou *des entêtes; — une plus (moins) value* ou *une plusvalue— moinsvalue, des plus (moins) value* ou *des plusvalues, moinsvalues; — un gallo romain* ou *un galloromain, des gallo romains* ou *des galloromains.*

Il est inutile de s'occuper du mot *sot l'y laisse,* si étrangement formé.

D'une manière générale, il est inutile de compliquer l'enseignement élémentaire et les exercices du pluriel des noms composés tels que *laisser aller, ouï dire,* qui, à cause de leur signification, ne s'emploient pas au pluriel.

Trait d'union. — Même quand les éléments constitutifs des noms composés seront séparés dans l'écriture, on n'exigera jamais de trait d'union.

ARTICLE

Article devant les noms propres de personnes. — L'usage existe d'employer l'article devant certains noms de famille italiens: *le Tasse, le Corrège,* et quelquefois à tort devant les prénoms: *(le) Dante, (le) Guide.* — On ne comptera pas comme faute l'ignorance de cet usage.

Il règne aussi une grande incertitude dans la manière d'écrire l'article qui fait partie de certains noms propres français: *la Fontaine* ou *Lafontaine, la Fayette* ou *Lafayette.* Il convient d'indiquer, dans les textes dictés, si, dans les noms propres qui contiennent un article, l'article doit être séparé du nom.

Article supprimé. — Lorsque deux adjectifs unis par *et* se rapportent au même substantif de manière à désigner en réalité deux choses différentes, on tolérera la suppression de l'article devant le second adjectif. Ex.: *l'histoire ancienne et moderne,* comme *l'histoire ancienne et la moderne.*

Article partitif. — On tolérera *du, de la, des,* au lieu de *de* partitif, devant un substantif précédé d'un adjectif. Ex.: *de* ou *du bon pain, de bonne viande* ou *de la bonne viande, de* ou *des bons fruits.*

Article devant *plus, moins,* etc. — La règle qui veut qu'on emploie *le plus, le moins, le mieux,* comme un neutre invariable devant un adjectif indiquant le degré le plus élevé de la qualité possédée par le substantif, qualifié sans comparaison avec d'autres objets, est très subtile et de peu d'utilité. Il est superflu de s'en occuper dans l'enseignement élémentaire et dans les exercices. On tolérera *le plus, la plus, les plus, les moins, les mieux,* etc., dans des constructions telles que: *on a abattu les arbres le plus* ou *les plus exposés à la tempête.*

Adjectif

Accord de l'adjectif. — Dans la locution *se faire fort de,* on tolérera l'accord de l'adjectif. Ex.: *se faire fort, forte, forts, fortes de* . . .

Adjectif construit avec plusieurs substantifs. — Lorsqu'un adjectif qualificatif suit plusieurs substantifs de genres différents, on tolérera toujours que l'adjectif soit construit au masculin pluriel, quel que soit le genre du substantif le plus voisin. Ex.: *appartements et chambres meublés.* — On tolérera aussi l'accord avec le substantif le plus rapproché. Ex.: *un courage et une foi nouvelle.*

Nu, demi, feu. — On tolérera l'accord de ces adjectifs avec le substantif qu'ils précèdent. Ex.: *nu* ou *nu pieds, une demi* ou *demie heure* (sans trait d'union entre les mots), *feu* ou *feue la reine.*

Adjectifs composés. — On tolérera la réunion des deux mots constitutifs en un seul mot, qui formera son féminin et son pluriel d'après la règle générale. Ex.: *nouveauné, nouveaunée, nouveaunés, nouveaunées; courtvêtu, courtvêtue, courtvêtus, courtvêtues,* etc.

Mais les adjectifs composés qui désignent des nuances étant devenus, par suite d'une ellipse, de véritables substantifs invariables, on les traitera comme des mots invariables. Ex.: *des robes bleu clair, vert d'eau,* etc., de même qu'on dit *des habits marron.*

Participes passés invariables. — Actuellement les participes *approuvé, attendu, ci-inclus, ci-joint, excepté, non compris, y compris, ôté, passé, supposé, vu,* placés avant le substantif auquel ils sont joints, restent invariables. *Excepté* est même déjà classé parmi les prépositions. On tolérera l'accord facultatif pour ces participes, sans exiger l'application de règles différentes suivant que ces mots sont placés au commencement ou dans le corps de la proposition, suivant que le substantif est ou n'est pas déterminé. Ex.: *ci joint* ou *ci jointes les pièces demandées* (sans trait d'union entre *ci* et le participe); — *je vous envoie ci joint* ou *ci jointe copie de la pièce.*
On tolérera la même liberté pour l'adjectif *franc.* Ex.: *envoyer franc de port* ou *franche de port une lettre.*

Avoir l'air. — On permettra d'écrire indifféremment: *elle a l'air doux* ou *douce, spirituel* ou *spirituelle.* On n'exigera pas la connaissance d'une différence de sens subtile suivant l'accord de l'adjectif avec le mot *air* ou avec le mot désignant la personne dont on indique l'air.

Adjectifs numéraux. — *Vingt, cent.* La prononciation justifie dans certains cas la règle actuelle, qui donne un pluriel à ces deux mots quand ils sont multipliés par un autre nombre. On tolérera le pluriel de *vingt* et de *cent,* même lorsque ces mots sont suivis d'un autre adjectif numéral. Ex.: *quatre vingt* ou *quatre vingts dix hommes;* — *quatre cent* ou *quatre cents trente hommes.*
Le trait d'union ne sera pas exigé entre le mot désignant les unités et le mot désignant les dizaines. Ex.: *dix sept.*
Dans la désignation du millésime, on tolérera *mille* au lieu de *mil,* comme dans l'expression d'un nombre. Ex.: *l'an mil huit cent quatre vingt dix* ou *l'an mille huit cents quatre vingts dix.*

Adjectifs démonstratifs, indéfinis et Pronoms

Ce. — On tolérera la réunion des particules *ci* et *là* avec le pronom qui les précède, sans exiger qu'on distingue *qu'est ceci, qu'est cela* de *qu'est ce ci, qu'est ce là.* — On tolérera la suppression du trait d'union dans ces constructions.

Même. — Après un substantif ou un pronom au pluriel, on tolérera l'accord de *même* au pluriel et on n'exigera pas de trait d'union entre *même* et le pronom. Ex.: *nous mêmes, les dieux mêmes.*

Tout. — On tolérera l'accord du mot *tout* aussi bien devant les adjectifs féminins commençant par une voyelle ou par une *h* muette que devant les adjectifs féminins commençant par une consonne ou par une *h* aspirée. Ex.: *des personnes tout heureuses* ou *toutes heureuses;* — *l'assemblée tout entière* ou *toute entière.*
Devant un nom de ville on tolérera l'accord du mot *tout* avec le nom propre, sans chercher à établir une différence un peu subtile entre des constructions comme *toute Rome* et *tout Rome.*

On ne comptera pas de faute non plus à ceux qui écriront indifféremment, en faisant parler une femme, *je suis tout à vous* ou *je suis toute à vous*.

Lorsque *tout* est employé avec le sens indéfini de *chaque*, on tolérera indifféremment la construction au singulier ou au pluriel du mot *tout* et du substantif qu'il accompagne. Ex.: *des marchandises de toute sorte* ou *de toutes sortes; — la sottise est de tout (tous) temps et de tout (tous) pays.*

Aucun. — Avec une négation, on tolérera l'emploi de ce mot aussi bien au pluriel qu'au singulier. Ex.: *ne faire aucun projet* ou *aucuns projets.*

Chacun. — Lorsque ce pronom est construit après le verbe et se rapporte à un mot pluriel sujet ou complément, on tolérera indifféremment, après *chacun*, le possessif *son, sa, ses* ou le possessif *leur, leurs*. Ex.: *ils sont sortis chacun de son côté* ou *de leur côté; — remettre des livres chacun à sa place* ou *à leur place.*

VERBE

Verbes composés. — On tolérera la suppression de l'apostrophe et du trait d'union dans les verbes composés. Ex.: *entrouvrir, entrecroiser.*

Trait d'union. — On tolérera l'absence de trait d'union entre le verbe et le pronom sujet placé après le verbe. Ex.: *est il?*

Différence du sujet apparent et du sujet réel. — Ex.: *sa maladie sont des vapeurs.* Il n'y a pas lieu d'enseigner de règles pour des constructions semblables, dont l'emploi ne peut être étudié utilement que dans la lecture et l'explication des textes. C'est une question de style et non de grammaire, qui ne saurait figurer ni dans les exercices élémentaires ni dans les examens.

Accord du verbe précédé de plusieurs sujets non unis par la conjonction et. — Si les sujets ne sont pas résumés par un mot indéfini tel que *tout, rien, chacun*, on tolérera toujours la construction du verbe au pluriel. Ex.: *sa bonté, sa douceur le font admirer.*

Accord du verbe précédé de plusieurs sujets au singulier unis par *ni*, *comme, avec, ainsi que* et autres locutions équivalentes. — On tolérera toujours le verbe au pluriel. Ex.: *ni la douceur ni la force n'y peuvent rien* ou *n'y peut rien; — la santé comme la fortune demandent à être ménagées* ou *demande à être ménagée; — le général avec quelques officiers sont sortis* ou *est sorti du camp; — le chat ainsi que le tigre sont des carnivores* ou *est un carnivore.*

Accord du verbe quand le sujet est un mot collectif. — Toutes les fois que le collectif est accompagné d'un complément au pluriel, on tolérera l'accord du verbe avec le complément. Ex.: *un peu de connaissances suffit* ou *suffisent.*

Accord du verbe quand le sujet est *plus d'un*. — L'usage actuel étant de construire le verbe au singulier avec le sujet *plus d'un*, on tolérera la construction du verbe au singulier, même lorsque *plus d'un* est suivi d'un complément au pluriel. Ex.: *plus d'un de ces hommes était* ou *étaient à plaindre.*

Accord du verbe précédé de *un de ceux* (*une de celles*) *qui.* — Dans quels cas le verbe de la proposition relative doit-il être construit au pluriel, et dans quels cas au singulier? C'est une délicatesse de langage qu'on n'essayera pas d'introduire dans les exercices élémentaires ni dans les examens.

C'est, ce sont. — Comme il règne une grande diversité d'usage relativement à l'emploi régulier de *c'est* et de *ce sont*, et que les meilleurs auteurs ont employé *c'est* pour annoncer un substantif au pluriel ou un pronom de la troisième personne au pluriel, on tolérera dans tous les cas l'emploi de *c'est* au lieu de *ce sont*. Ex.: *c'est* ou *ce sont des montagnes et des précipices.*

Concordance ou correspondance des temps. — On tolérera le présent du subjonctif au lieu de l'imparfait dans les propositions subordonnées dépendant de propositions dont le verbe est au conditionnel. Ex.: *il faudrait qu'il vienne* ou *qu'il vînt.*

PARTICIPE

Participe présent et adjectif verbal. — Il convient de s'en tenir à la règle générale d'après laquelle on distingue le participe de l'adjectif en ce que le premier indique l'action, et le second l'état. Il suffit que les élèves et les candidats fassent preuve de bons sens dans les cas douteux. On devra éviter avec soin les subtilités dans les exercices. Ex.: *des sauvages vivent errant* ou *errants dans les bois.*

Participe passé. — La règle d'accord enseignée actuellement à propos du participe passé construit avec l'auxiliaire *avoir* a toujours été plus ou moins contestée par les écrivains et par les grammairiens. Peu à peu, elle s'est compliquée de plus en plus; les exceptions sont devenues de plus en plus nombreuses, suivant la forme du complément qui précède le participe, suivant que le même verbe est employé au sens propre ou au sens figuré, suivant que d'autres verbes accompagnent le participe. En outre, elle tombe en désuétude. Il paraît inutile de s'obstiner à maintenir artificiellement une règle qui n'est qu'une cause d'embarras dans l'enseignement, qui ne sert à rien pour le développement de l'intelligence, et qui rend très difficile l'étude du français aux étrangers.

Il n'y a rien à changer à la règle d'après laquelle le participe passé construit comme épithète doit s'accorder avec le mot qualifié, et construit comme attribut avec le verbe *être* ou un verbe intransitif doit s'accorder avec le sujet. Ex.: *des fruits gâtés; — ils sont tombés; — elles sont tombées.*

Pour le participe passé construit avec l'auxiliaire *avoir*, on tolérera qu'il reste invariable dans tous les cas où on prescrit aujourd'hui de le faire accorder avec le complément. Ex.: *les livres que j'ai lu* ou *lus; — les fleurs qu'elles ont cueilli* ou *cueillies; — la peine que j'ai pris* ou *prise.*

Pour le participe passé des verbes réfléchis, on tolérera aussi qu'il reste invariable dans tous les cas où on prescrit aujourd'hui de le faire accorder. Ex.: *elles se sont tu* ou *tues; — les coups que nous nous sommes donné* ou *donnés.*

ADVERBE

Ne **dans les propositions subordonnées.** — L'emploi de cette négation dans un très grand nombre de propositions subordonnées donne lieu à des règles compliquées, difficiles, abusives, souvent en contradiction avec l'usage des écrivains les plus classiques.

Sans faire de règles différentes suivant que les propositions dont elles dépendent sont affirmatives ou négatives ou interrogatives, on tolérera la suppression de la négation *ne* dans les propositions subordonnées dépendant de verbes ou de locutions signifiant:

Empêcher, défendre, éviter que, etc.   Ex.: *défendre qu'on vienne* ou *qu'on ne vienne;*

Craindre, désespérer, avoir peur, de peur que, etc.   Ex.: *de peur qu'il aille* ou *qu'il n'aille;*

Douter, contester, nier que, etc.   Ex.: *je ne doute pas que la chose soit vraie* ou *ne soit vraie;*

Il tient à peu, il ne tient pas à, il s'en faut que, etc.   Ex.: *il ne tient pas à moi que cela se fasse* ou *ne se fasse.*

On tolérera de même la suppression de cette négation après les comparatifs et les mots indiquant une comparaison: *autre, autrement que,* etc.   Ex.: *l'année a été meilleure qu'on l'espérait* ou *qu'on ne l'espérait; — les résultats sont autres qu'on le croyait* ou *qu'on ne le croyait.*

De même, après les locutions *à moins que, avant que.* Ex.: *à moins qu'on accorde le pardon* ou *qu'on n'accorde le pardon.*

OBSERVATION

Il conviendra, dans les examens, de ne pas compter comme fautes graves celles qui ne prouvent rien contre l'intelligence et le véritable savoir des candidats, mais qui prouvent seulement l'ignorance de quelque finesse ou de quelque subtilité grammaticale. Ainsi, notamment, il conviendra de compter très légèrement: 1° les fautes portant sur les substantifs qui changent de genre suivant qu'ils sont employés au sens abstrait ou au sens concret, tels que *aide, garde, manœuvre,* etc., ou qui changent légèrement de sens en changeant de genre, tels que *couple, merci, relâche,* etc.; — 2° les fautes relatives au pluriel spécial de certains substantifs, particulièrement dans les langues techniques, tels que *aïeuls* et *aïeux, ciels* et *cieux, œils* et *yeux, travails* et *travaux,* etc.; — 3° les fautes relatives à l'emploi ou à la suppression de l'article ou à l'emploi de prépositions différentes devant les noms propres masculins désignant des pays.   Ex.: *aller en Danemark, en Portugal,* mais *aller au Japon, au Brésil.*

INDEX

An index of subject matter and proper names occurring in the text and notes. Bibliography at end of chapters and all individual words are *not* listed. References are to pages.